ROUTLEDGE LIBRARY EDITIO
ECONOMICS AND SOCIETY

Volume 30

SOCIAL ECONOMICS

SOCIAL ECONOMICS

J. HARRY JONES

Routledge
Taylor & Francis Group
LONDON AND NEW YORK

First published in 1922 by Methuen & Co. Ltd.

This edition first published in 2026
by Routledge
4 Park Square, Milton Park, Abingdon, Oxon OX14 4RN

and by Routledge
605 Third Avenue, New York, NY 10158

Routledge is an imprint of the Taylor & Francis Group, an informa business

British Library Cataloguing in Publication Data
A catalogue record for this book is available from the British Library

ISBN: 978-1-032-97576-4 (Set)
ISBN: 978-1-041-14095-5 (Volume 30) (hbk)
ISBN: 978-1-041-14096-2 (Volume 30) (pbk)
ISBN: 978-1-003-67295-1 (Volume 30) (ebk)

DOI: 10.4324/9781003672951

Publisher's Note
The publisher has gone to great lengths to ensure the quality of this reprint but points out that some imperfections in the original copies may be apparent.

Disclaimer
The publisher has made every effort to trace copyright holders and would welcome correspondence from those they have been unable to trace.

SOCIAL ECONOMICS

BY

J. HARRY JONES, M.A.

PROFESSOR OF ECONOMICS IN THE UNIVERSITY OF LEEDS
ONE TIME FELLOW OF THE UNIVERSITY OF WALES

AUTHOR OF 'THE TINPLATE INDUSTRY'
'ECONOMICS OF WAR AND CONQUEST' ETC.

SECOND EDITION

METHUEN & CO. LTD.
36 ESSEX STREET W.C.
LONDON

First Published . . . April 29th 1920
Second Edition . . . March 1922

TO

MY FRIEND

L. L. PRICE

b

PREFACE

THIS book is "full of omissions." It became necessary to make a choice between the early publication of a brief survey of the most important and urgent problems of economic reorganisation and the later publication of a lengthy treatment of such problems, the latter to include closer discussions of suggested solutions. The interest shown by Glasgow audiences at public lectures in the winter and spring (when I was lecturer in Social Economics in the University of Glasgow) seemed to me to suggest that the former might prove of greater value. The chief difficulty thus lay not in writing, but afterwards in reducing the size of a book which quickly grew too large to make any appeal to the general reader. This must be my apology for the omissions, and also for the absence of any attempt to justify the choice of title.

I have endeavoured to emphasise the interrelations of individual economic and social problems in such a way as to bring out the central economic problem, which may be crudely described as the reconciliation of individual ambition and social welfare. That it is of the first importance, for example, to discuss financial problems in terms of labour and labour problems in terms of currency is clearly shown in the two strikes which have been declared since the last chapter of the book was written—first the moulders' strike and now the railwaymen's strike.

I desire to acknowledge my indebtedness to my friend Mrs. G. Power, who read most of the chapters in manuscript and offered suggestions which were in all cases adopted.

J. H. JONES

OXFORD, *September* 1919

NOTE TO SECOND EDITION

APART from minor corrections, no change has been made in the present edition. The book deals mainly with principles, and these do not appear to have been affected by the important events which have occurred since it was first issued. In the coal industry the natural region (as advocated in these pages) has been accepted as the unit of control, and an experiment in profit-sharing has been started which may prove to be the most significant industrial event of the present century; but longer experience, and experience under normal conditions, must be acquired before many useful generalisations can be made. Sufficient has already become known, however, to illustrate the value of publicity in industrial affairs, and to add strength to some of the conclusions on the subject which appear in this volume. In the engineering industries questions of "sovereignty" or "management" have arisen which provide striking illustration of the statements contained in Chapter VII. The recent history of Trade Boards seems to me to point to the possibility of substantial improvement in the machinery of conciliation and arbitration. But consideration of such questions would have involved the addition of many pages to a volume already sufficiently large. Again, the post-armistice boom in trade has been followed by profound depression. But the depression, probably intensified by the action (or in-action) of the Government and of municipal authorities, is mainly due to international factors. Adequate examination of the problem can only be made as part of a study of international economics, and a supplementary volume on this subject is now being written. For these reasons it was decided to publish the present edition without material alterations.

J. H. J.

March 1922

CONTENTS

SOCIAL ECONOMICS

CHAPTER I

GROWTH OF THE MODERN INDUSTRIAL PROBLEM

THE organisation of economic society is based upon co-operation. Co-operation is anterior to and more fundamental than competition. Competition is not the negation of co-operation; it is the form of expression which the co-operative principle assumes at a certain stage of economic development. Economic development, again, may be thought of as the increase of complexity in the forms which co-operation takes, with the consequent emergence of new economic functions. Many social problems simply mirror the problems which every organisation—be it church, army, or political government—creates as it becomes more complex. And the heart of a social problem resides not in difficulty of function so much as in the responsibility of every part for the welfare of the organic whole.

Co-operation may be a temporary and simple supplement to individual economy, as in the case of two men rowing a boat, or several men working in a hayfield. But, had it never passed this stage, co-operation would have proved a poor handmaiden of progress. Even in its earliest development it took a more complex form, supplanting rather than merely supplementing individual economy, which thus became the exception rather than the rule. Groups of independent workmen gave place to bands of specialised workers, whose different but correlated activities still required but little skill and few tools. The change represented a distinct advance. Command over nature was increased, and better living conditions brought within reach. Further, the aggregate group was welded into an organisation conscious of its parts and sensitive to their welfare. Not yet, perhaps, a highly nervous organism, but a body economic, with interdependent members. It is known in history as the village community.

This body economic, simple though it was, had its own problems to face. It declared against communism and in favour of the exchange system, thus mobilising the most fundamental—and therefore universal—of human characteristics, the love of distinction and variety. Co-operation was thus early based upon the appeal to individual gain, and thus incidentally called into being one of the greatest economic instruments ever invented, money, or medium of exchange, which merely represents the power to command the products of other men's labour. The problems of this simple society were not those of industrialism in the modern sense. There were rich and poor, and class distinctions: but there were no conflicts between 'capital' and 'labour,' for capitalists and wage-earners, as the terms are now generally used, did not yet exist. Trading was a simple but laborious function. The youth served his apprenticeship to an industry. He became an improver, then a journeyman, and in most cases realised his ambition by becoming a master-craftsman. In those days there was always room at the top, and to reach it little capital was required, as the instruments of production were still in a simple and elementary stage. But with the growth of the small economic group master-craftsmen increased in number, and their rivalry, in a money economy, began to take the form which we now call competition. Guilds of master-craftsmen, or craft-guilds, as they were called, complained of the intrusion of interlopers, who paid little or no respect to custom and tradition. Trade rivalries were set up, which incidentally stimulated progress and unconsciously served the interests of economic society by applying the principle of specialisation to individual trades and industries. The master-craftsman now employed a number of workers, who were journeymen wage-earners. These divided among them the whole range of operations forming a craft, each worker performing his own special part and that alone. The system of large though still 'domestic' factories and workshops thus came gradually into prominence, and produced far-reaching results.

First among these may be noted the effect upon the apprenticeship system. At an earlier stage of its development the young apprentice was taught the whole of a craft, and, as he lived in or near his master's house, his industrial conduct and general manners were continuously under careful supervision. His training over, he was assured of a career determined mainly by his skill and industry. Historical monographs, moreover, convey the impression that the master had a daughter of suitable age for whom the good apprentice ultimately conceived an affection. Having married the daughter he succeeded, in due course, to the master's business. The less fortunate apprentices whose training took place too early or too late in the daughter's life could at least start for themselves as independent craftsmen, since they had practised the whole range of operations constituting their particular craft. In those industries in which internal organisation was based upon specialisation of function, apprenticeship tended to become unsatisfactory. Training was too specialised, control lax, and openings as journeymen difficult to find.

The second result of the 'domestic' factory system was closely connected with the first, and consisted in the emergence of two distinct classes—employers and wage-earners. As the master-craftsmen now employed a large number of workers, it is obvious that there was not room at the top for all of them. Moreover, the amount of material used, and of money required for wages and simple tools, was already so great that only those in command of a relatively large capital could hope to become masters. It is true that, then as now, any journeyman could become an independent master-craftsman on a small scale. If he showed exceptional skill and enterprise he might even achieve success; but, from the nature of the case, such a man would be the exception rather than the rule. Thus inevitably grew up a *class* of life-long wage-earners, whose interests differed widely from the interests of those earlier journeymen who normally became small masters. The formation of two distinctive and separate classes—employers and wage-earners—with divergent if not conflicting interests, created the 'labour problem.' The consequent need for a class organisation differing essentially from the obsolete trade guilds became clamant, and the trade union emerged to protect the common interests of the class of industrial workers. But although the need for trade unions was apparent under the 'domestic' system of industry, and a number of local unions were formed, the opportunity for thoroughgoing organisation had not yet come.

The third consequence of specialisation which calls for reference at this stage is the substitution of machinery for hand labour and the growth of the modern factory system. The more a craftsman's function was split up into parts, and the smaller the number of operations each worker was allowed to perform, the more mechanical and narrow did the work become. It is only when work becomes entirely mechanical that it can be performed by machinery. The so-called 'industrial revolution' between 1760 and 1820 represented a series of inventions—and their application to industry—which followed naturally upon the specialism of the preceding century of sectionalised operations. To strain a metaphor, machinery was in the air before it was planted on the ground. The most mechanical form of effort is the provision of power. In primitive times beasts of burden were used. When the wheel was discovered, many of these were harnessed and employed in transport. Water was soon seized upon for the provision of power in the factories, and later, the value of steam in this connection was discovered. Other inventions were made *pari passu,* and by the close of the European War the factory containing steam-driven hammers and machinery was within sight. Impelled, if not compelled, by industrial rivalry or competition, employers sought and discovered means of securing greater results from a given expenditure of human effort. Command over nature was increased: natural forces were harnessed to secure the conquest; and the competitors themselves unconsciously co-operated. While working for themselves they worked also for a society which attached supreme importance to the growth of material wealth—the tangible reward of wresting nature's secrets—but had not yet learnt to pay attention to the human balance sheet. Then, as now, those who sought economy through efficiency triumphed over those who sought efficiency through economy.

The growth of machine production led inevitably, under a competitive system, to very careful choice of factory sites. This would be necessary, indeed, under any system attaching great importance to economy of energy. But the mere installation of machinery involved outlay on fixed capital, and success or failure in the venture depended largely upon the extent to which natural facilities were utilised. Steam-driven factories and their workers thus tended to concentrate in coal-bearing areas. In many industries, moreover, factories showed a strong tendency to grow in size. Their number consequently diminished relatively to the market. These facts, which are merely noted at this stage, call for further attention in the chapter which follows. It is desirable first to consider certain other consequences of machine production, some of which appear inevitable, not merely under the present system, but under any system of economic organisation which can be devised. The home-worker, and even the wage-earner in a domestic factory, working independently and without mechanical aid, can arrange his working day with greater freedom than a factory worker. The factory worker (as in a rolling-mill, for example) may form one of a group. These workmen jointly and simultaneously produce a given result by the individual performance of different but related operations, utilising at the same time mechanical power obtained at relatively great expense. It is obvious that if the factory worker is to be an effective unit, his working day must be fitted into that of his colleagues. Regular hours thus became a necessity, and the factory whistle started its shrieking career. But regular hours came to mean long hours of work which, in the case of process workers, was practically continuous. Some processes were quite simple, and could be conducted, with but little practice, by young women and children. These were brought into the factories and mines and called upon to work under conditions determined by the owner. Carried along by the force of competition, owners constantly substituted cheaper for more expensive methods, and conserved energy by utilising skill to the uttermost. To this end they employed women and children as far and for as long as possible, and in most cases, under those objective conditions which cost least at the moment. This colossal evil was the first by-product of uncontrolled industrialism. During the nineteenth century the nation endeavoured to remove it by legislation regulating the conditions of employment of women and children. Long hours of uninterrupted toil, even for strong men, are now recognised to be not merely unprofitable, but socially disastrous. The importance of a new form of balance sheet is no longer denied. The fact remains, nevertheless, that regular hours, as distinguished from long hours, are inevitable, if the factory system is to be continued where it exists and developed in industries still carried on in workshops and the homes of the workers.

The purpose of invention and of improvements in industrial organisation is to conserve human energy by increasing the net result of human effort. In other words, it aims at reducing the expenditure of effort required to produce a given result. Substitution of better for worse methods involves the immediate displacement of labour which frequently either cannot or will not adapt itself to the new circumstances. The protest of the hand-loom weavers against the unemployment created by the introduction of the power-loom has quite recently been echoed by the glassblowers and sheet-metal workers. Nor are such groups impressed by the reply that there is room for all in the world of employment, and that economic progress cannot be achieved without individual hardship. They are mainly concerned with their own welfare, and they are taught by experience that the new forms of work which are offered (or discovered) are frequently of a type for which their own apprenticeship was no preparation. They also become aware that before the transference was complete employers in the first trade had taken advantage of the temporary glut to reduce wages, and that such reductions were readily accepted by most of the men as the lesser of two evils. Those employers, therefore, who sought efficiency through economy, continued to employ the older methods by sweated labour, and retarded the development of better methods. The men frequently lost both ways. It is therefore little wonder that, apart from special cases which will call for observation in the chapter on labour organisation, the apprenticeship system lost its popularity among the workers and fell into desuetude. Of what avail years spent in expensive and laborious preparation if in the end the trade itself disappeared, or shrank to such an extent that it offered but a poor and precarious living? [1] A tendency to eliminate skilled workers

[1] The results of technical improvements within a factory were also sometimes produced by the transference of industries from one region to another. The classic example is, of course, the decay of agriculture in this country during the last half-century. But migrations also occur from one part of the country to another, as in

and to substitute machinery operated by semi-skilled or unskilled workers appears even yet at first sight in some industries. And appearance is not wholly false. The conservation of human energy by the substitution of machinery for hand labour, or by the improvement of machinery itself does in some cases tend to reduce the amount of skilled labour relatively to unskilled labour employed. But this tendency may reach a point beyond which it is no longer operative. Thus machine tools are invented which can be worked by youths and girls under the supervision of a skilled tool-setter. These tools are in turn supplanted by automatic machines which dispense with the need of unskilled workers. The first effect of the introduction of machinery is to necessitate the employment of people on comparatively unskilled work. But as that work becomes more and more mechanical it is absorbed by machinery (witness the substitution of electrical machines for men feeding steel furnaces) and the proportion of unskilled labour required is reduced rather than further increased. But it is not sufficient merely to fix attention upon process workers employed on a plant. Every considerable improvement of machinery and enlargement of plant calls for an increase in the number of indirect workers, such as mill engineers, cranemen, joiners, repairers, etc., most of whom are skilled craftsmen. Moreover, the commercial and managerial functions of the enterprise become more exacting and absorb a relatively larger amount of labour. Finally, new industries are created and others become relatively more important. If a nation enjoys real economic progress, purely manufacturing industries begin to absorb a diminishing

the gradual tendency of the steel industry to leave inland places for the seaboard.

proportion of its total labour force. Thus, while it may be true that in some industries the demand for unskilled workers is growing relatively to the demand for skilled workers, and that in more cases skilled craftsmen employed in particular trades are *relatively* less in demand, it is at least doubtful if the proportion of labour as a whole which is required for unskilled work is on the increase.

It has been stated that the need for labour organisation first appeared when specialisation of work within a trade created two distinct classes, employers and wage-earners, with distinct and frequently conflicting interests. The real opportunity to form associations appeared with the growth of factories. When men worked in isolation, or in small isolated groups which rarely met, the difficulty of maintaining continuous associations proved so great as to prevent their rapid growth. But when men began to work together in large numbers, and similar factories were concentrated in one small area, the prospect of successful association grew much brighter and a small wave of unionism spread over the country. This was followed, during the nineteenth century, by other larger and stronger waves until, at the time when the World War broke out, the labour movement was perhaps the strongest single force in the country. But during the greater part of the Industrial Revolution, when the beneficial effect of technical progress appeared to be its only effect, such organisations were regarded as a hindrance, and in 1799 were declared to be illegal. The workers, however, were not to be denied. Driven largely by the fear of unemployment, or at the least, of reductions of wages forced upon them by unprogressive employers striving to compete with enterprising rivals who had adopted the new methods, they formed societies which were ostensibly only friendly societies, but which were also in part societies for the protection of their common interests as wage-earners. So strong was the revolt against the combination (or anti-combination) laws that these were finally repealed in 1824.

Technical improvements have not only followed and been followed by division of labour in a horizontal direction, but have resulted in cross-sections or vertical divisions of processes into distinct and separate industries. The chain of production has been considerably lengthened in some cases, and many of the workers are far removed from the final products, which may be of many kinds. A machine tool, for example, is made from steel castings obtained from the foundry; the castings are made from steel manufactured at the steel works from pig-iron produced at the blast furnace; and the iron is obtained by burning coke, limestone and iron ore. But iron, steel and coal are also used for many other purposes. Thus industry may be regarded as a maze, containing many focussing points and points of bifurcation. Many of these represent industries producing highly standardised products, the producing units being relatively large.

The majority of manufacturing and transport industries present common features which call for observation. Not only do the men perform a definitely restricted task, but the output of the factory as a whole may be only one part of a finished product, or represent only one stage in its manufacture. It is therefore not to be expected that the workmen should manifest the same interest in such work as is felt by the craftsman who shares with the artist the joy of creative effort. Congenial work is welcome to most people, for too much leisure makes for boredom and unhappiness. But the kind of work daily performed by a large proportion of factory employees is, in a sense, forced labour. They have no choice in the matter except the power of selection among a small group of occupations with the same essential features. Unlike professional work, industrial work holds little or no interest within itself, and is therefore toilsome. Coal mining, for example, can never be made pleasant. The point is one which requires emphasis to-day, for there is strong evidence in support of the view that industrial unrest represents in part a reaction or revolt against industrialism itself, not merely a protest against low wages, undesirable conditions of employment, or the system of private ownership and competition. It is probable, too, that this revolt owes much of its strength to the vague feeling that a change in the economic system will somehow or other effect a change in the nature of industrial work itself, or at least in that part of it which the individual worker will be required to perform.

The lengthening of the chain of production has also enormously complicated the problem of providing continuous employment for the workers. The need for the products of any industry depends ultimately upon the need of society for the finished goods which the workers are instrumental in making. The demand for bricks, for example, is determined in the last resort by the demand for houses and other structures. But demand must be anticipated and prepared for, and the actual position of any industry depends not upon the requirements of other industries at the same time, but upon the present estimate of their future requirements. During the nineteenth century the trade forecasts of employers were no more reliable than the weather forecasts of meteorologists, and frequent errors were made. An error in one direction meant scarcity, high prices and overtime ; in the other a glut, low prices and unemployment. A marked feature of nineteenth-century trade was its alternate expansion and contraction. Booms and depressions followed each other with such extreme regularity that the alternating periods were called ' cycles,' the very periodicity of which suggested a clue to their explanation.

Technical improvements and the geographic concentration of industry are conditioned by transport facilities. Where such facilities do not exist, industry must be widely distributed, each part supplying the local market and remaining small and relatively unprogressive. The steady growth of transport agencies during the last two centuries encouraged market expansion. Machine production was thus facilitated, and manufacturing industries concentrated in suitable but relatively small and few areas. This development has in turn reacted upon transport. Older and smaller economic regions have thus lost their independence in respect of the necessaries of life, and are linked together to form a larger economic unit : interlocal, interregional and international trade has assumed an importance of a different kind from that which it enjoyed in earlier centuries. The growth of transport by road, rail and sea has also called into existence a large body of workers whose task it is to load and unload. The work of those employed at docks in the loading and unloading of ships is intermittent owing to the comparative uncertainty of shipping time-tables. Consequently, as the shipping industry grew more important in the national economy, the problem of casual labour—that is, labour which, neither in theory nor in practice, is assured of continuous employment—became more important and urgent. On the old materialistic balance sheet of the nineteenth century, when cost meant immediate money cost, the organisation of casual labour so as to promote greater continuity of work would appear only as an item on the liability side. Casual labour was cheap labour, and therefore, by implication, a desirable form of labour. As the greater part of such work called for little or no skill, those who failed in industries providing more continuous employment gravitated, in coastal regions, towards the docks, where there were always more applicants than jobs. Efforts have been made in recent years, particularly in London and Liverpool, to decasualise such labour at the ports, but in spite of the success of some of these efforts the problem remains among the most urgent and difficult of solution. And the problem is not merely to decasualise port labour, but to guarantee continuity of employment in all industries. Under peace conditions even a skilled engineer employed in a large engineering establishment on the Clyde might be told by his foreman at four o'clock that his services would not be required after five. If trade happened to be slack at the moment this form of dismissal was frequently employed. The foreman knew that as soon as trade improved he would be able to select a competent worker from among the applicants at the gate. To the firm this was a cheap method of organising labour force, but to the average worker it gave a feeling of insecurity which was never absent. For although statistics could be marshalled to show that the number who actually suffered in this way was but a small percentage of the total number employed, the individual worker of average ability—

unlike Adam Smith's employer who believed in his own good fortune—felt keenly that he himself might prove to be the foreman's victim. In the South Wales tinplate industry (and in most branches of domestic service) a worker is entitled to a month's notice of dismissal; and the difficulties which would be encountered in making this system general are not of the first importance.

The growth of the industrial unit and the geographic concentration of industry, combined with what has been called the lengthening of the chain of production, in which each link forms an industry by itself, has meant that economic areas have ceased to be self-supporting. They are now interdependent and form an organic whole, the parts of which are linked up by an elaborate system of transport to which reference has already been made. But the new organisation has also brought into prominence a group of important and special functions which are usually denoted by the term 'commerce.' Commerce is concerned with the buying and selling of goods and with the necessary arrangements for their transport. While many urge that this function has hitherto been inadequately performed, or performed by a disproportionate expenditure of human effort, it is in itself a necessary function. Moreover, it is certain that wise prevision or intelligent speculation, which forms part of it, has a stabilising rather than a disturbing effect upon industry and economic society generally. As the business unit increases and large aggregates of men or goods or enterprises come under consideration, losses, errors and accidents appear with regularity and inevitability. It is possible therefore to estimate these in advance, and to make joint provision for or against them. This provision, which is called insur-

ate increase in the number of children reared amid evil conditions, and a less than proportionate increase in the number of youths who will be able to share in the real benefits of town life. It is important, therefore, that the causes of concentration of population should be examined.

Population follows industry, or has an industrial basis. The geographic distribution of some industries carries with it an obvious explanation. Many services are essentially ' local.' Such are the provision of gas and electricity; tramways and light railways; road-making; cleansing; domestic and other personal services, such as hair-dressing; the distributive trades with their ancillary occupations; the provision of amusements, and the exercise of many professions and arts. All these ultimately depend upon the manufacture by specialised industries of products which are sold outside the industrial region. Every factory erected or mine opened calls for a considerable increase in the supply of such subsidiary services. But the prosperity of the region is bound up with the prosperity of the industries which supply extra-local needs; and if for any reason these disappeared, it is literally true to say that the region would shrivel up like Rider Haggard's Ayesha. The means of rendering payment for the ' imported ' food, clothing and other necessary and desirable things would be lacking, and the people would need to move on to other regions. There would be no means of securing a living except by the return to a self-sufficing regional economy. This would be impossible for more than a fraction of the population, and even for these the standard of living would be very low.

The problem of localisation is therefore chiefly important in respect of those industries which are specialised in the above sense. The distribution of some of these is self-explanatory. Mining can only be carried on where coal and metalliferous ores are known to exist ; quarrying where there is stone, ironstone, limestone or clay ; agriculture and fruit-farming where the soil is favourable ; fishing in certain well-defined coastal areas. Health and holiday resorts thrive because they provide service, on the spot, to visitors or retired residents who bring means of payment from outside ; large ports like Liverpool are great distributive centres and ' export ' to other areas services for which payment is made (little wonder that during the war Hamburg was like a city of the dead !) ; Edinburgh is typical of the city which provides administrative and professional services to a large outside community. Parasitism among cities does not, therefore, exist, unless we assume that only concrete goods should count in the world market as value received.

Examination of the forces determining the distribution or concentration of manufacturing industries almost necessarily involves the recognition of two important distinctions. The first of these is the distinction between the original causes which created an industry and gave it an early momentum on the one hand, and, on the other, those consequences of early growth which explain its permanence and expansion even when the original causes of its existence have themselves disappeared. The second distinction is that between those forces which determine the large region most suitable for a given industry and those local factors, such as local rates, water-supply, railway facilities, the lie of the land, etc., which determine the exact spot within a region suitable for the erection of one factory or a group of factories. Local factors of the last kind are largely under human control, and are therefore susceptible of variation. It is here that the study of regionalism and the carrying out of regional surveys may prove an effective instrument of social progress.

The original causes leading to the selection of any area for the establishment of a manufacturing industry may be one or more of many. Certain industries may be traditionally or historically associated with particular areas. Others may have been established in some region where there was an adequate supply of the requisite kind of labour. Near Kilmarnock, for example, there is a flourishing lace-cotton industry which was created nearly a century ago when the local hand-loom weavers were displaced by power-looms. The location of some industries may even be traced to the personal factor. There appears to be little doubt that the education and initiative of German manufacturers have accounted in large measure for the growth of the chemical and spelter industries, although there were other forces at work.

It may confidently be stated, however, that the progress of industries which owe their origin to the causes already mentioned would have been arrested if other more important forces had not either operated in the same general direction or at least remained neutral. In general, there are three external forces in operation. Sometimes these concentrate upon a given region, sometimes they act in different—possibly opposite—directions. And the most economic site, or group of sites, for an industry represents the point of equilibrium of these forces. As they frequently change in strength and direction, the points of equilibrium are variable. These forces are the market, raw material and source of power—a

Big Three. Where the market is widely distributed, its influence is less than where it is concentrated. If it is overseas, there is a tendency, other things being equal, for the industry to move towards the coast, in order that the cost of railway transport may be eliminated or largely reduced. If a great part of its raw material is lost in process of manufacture, an industry has a marked tendency to establish itself near the place where the raw material is obtained. If, however, none is wasted, it is a matter of indifference at what point on a line drawn between its place of origin and the market for the manufactured article the industry is established. The more bulky the article and the more difficult to pack, the more pronounced will be the 'pull' of the market, particularly if the article is not standardised. But the strongest site-determining force is power. When factories were driven by water-power they were placed on the banks of streams possessing an adequate natural fall. During the nineteenth century steam was substituted for water, and falling streams lost their attraction. Coal, the new source of power, was completely destroyed in the performance of its single function. Mines thus proved a strong magnet to the manufacturing industries, and mining regions became also manufacturing regions. Further, coal was used not only as a source of power but also as a raw material in the manufacture of iron and steel, and as a generator of heat in all 'furnace' industries. For these reasons the metal trades found it doubly attractive, and for these reasons too mining regions showed a strong tendency during last century to become 'black countries.' This tendency was further strengthened where, as in the Clyde basin and the Cleveland district, iron ore was discovered in close proximity to coal

Here the cost of assembling materials which would not bear heavy transport charges was relatively small.

Young manufacturing districts tend to increase rapidly in size, and soot grows like a snowball. As soon as a foundation industry has made a real start, adequate railway and other transport facilities are provided, expert labour is trained, subsidiary trades are established, and the district enjoys a wider industrial basis. In time the subsidiary industries become specialised (witness the making of cotton machinery in and around Manchester) and the main industries themselves specialise more than at first, and flourish exceedingly. Thus an economic region may be rapidly transformed, and acquire a momentum which carries it far beyond the reach of the original cause of its growth. It may exhibit a great variety of industries, yet most, if not all, of these will, like the heavy trades of the west of Scotland, derive their prosperity from—even depend for their existence upon—one main industry. In any case green fields give place to tenements and dingy streets, filled with pallid and precocious children; blue skies are obscured by curtains of smoke, the air is polluted and smuts take the place of dew. And, instead of roses, green lawns and lusty youngsters, we contemplate columns of statistics revealing the extent of our prosperity, and imagine all is well. Then we develop champagne tastes while we still have only beer pockets, and exhibit signs of 'unrest.'

The growing use of electricity as the driving power of machinery brings fresh hope of improvement in industrial conditions. If the Coal Conservation Committee has not been the victim of blind optimism it is reasonable to believe that the forces making for geographic concentration of industry are rapidly losing strength. Electricity can apparently be conveyed a given distance much more cheaply than that quantity of coal which is necessary to produce equivalent power. If such is the case a strong force has been liberated to work for the decentralisation of industry. The tendency towards concentration is further checked by the growth of land values in urban areas. Scarcity of land leads to keen competition between potential users, and the price tends to rise to a level above which it is more economical to go farther afield. In seeking that level landlords frequently make individual errors, by which their very 'keenness' unintentionally serves the ultimate interests of the community. As things are they succeed, by the exercise of property rights acquired in earlier and less prosperous times, in transferring to themselves and the inheritors of their wealth a proportion of the beneficial results of industrial concentration. This is not an attack on landlords: the 'unearned increment' is already in existence: nor have the manufacturers or the workpeople as such any stronger claim upon it beyond that which comes with numbers. The higher the rental value the greater the probability, under the existing form of organisation (or any form which regards each parcel of land as a separate economic entity), that the land has been put to its best commercial use. It is not even a question of competition *versus* socialism, for a socialist State, having to decide whether it should aim at the greatest possible result from a given expenditure of human effort, and the provision of the service desired by the consumer at the lowest possible cost per unit, would find it difficult, if not impossible, to escape the dilemma.

The third force making for decentralisation is improvement in transport. Geographic concentration of industry is conditioned by facilities for transporting industrial products. It is found that if transport could be provided gratis and with the rapidity of lightning, it would cease to act as a force, and the location of industries would be determined by other factors, such as relative wages, climatic conditions and the like, with a strong tendency towards a wider distribution. A reduction in the net cost of transport thus acts as a double force, tending in some cases to greater and in others to less concentration. To take one example: it would arrest the tendency of export trades to leave the Midlands for the coast. Generally, too, it would tend to perpetuate industries already existing in those places where they have been established, mainly on account of the other facilities which have been created, and to which reference has already been made. But it is also extremely likely that places now regarded as inaccessible, or from which transport charges are deemed to be prohibitive, would be selected in preference to overcrowded regions. Devonshire and the Channel Islands are now among London's market-gardens. It may be suggested, as a rough generalisation, that at the present stage of progress improvements in transport tend to greater geographic concentration upon a comparatively large region, to greater diffusion within that region and an extension of the region itself. A moderate reduction in protective duties would tend to produce the same result as between large regions.

Industrial areas within this country have been allowed to develop without external control or inter-local barriers. Even internal or local regulation has been slight and more or less arbitrary. Some districts are richly endowed by nature, and appear the most suitable for industries which nevertheless do not flourish there. The home of cotton manufacture is East Lancashire, where one of the greatest attractions was the damp climate favourable for spinning fine counts. There is also a small textile industry in the Clyde valley, where the climate is damp enough to satisfy the most exacting manufacturer. Nor were the other advantages absent which were enjoyed by the Manchester district. Yet the Clyde textile industry shows no sign of rivalling the Lancashire industry. The explanation is comparatively simple. Like an individual, an economic region makes a choice of career fairly early in life, and generally clings to that career. Its population, and therefore its activity, is limited. It chooses the work it can do best, although it may be able to do other work better than those who actually carry it on. A business man may employ a clerk inferior to himself even in clerical work, thereby saving time which he devotes to higher and more remunerative forms of activity. A good bowler is often sent in to bat last in a cricket match even when he is a better batsman than other members of the side, because his value to the team is greater as a bowler, and may be seriously prejudiced if he tires himself making a large score. A versatile football player may be the best three-quarter-back on the side, but if his superiority is even more pronounced at half-back he will be of greatest service in that position. These illustrations are apt, for they present analogies. The superiority of the Clyde valley appeared in the circumstances to be greatest in respect of shipbuilding and its dependent industries, and in that group it sought a career. Similarly, part of South Wales, which is well suited to other metal trades, found its industrial career in the tinplate and galvanised sheet trades.

If a growing population cannot be fully absorbed by the main industries in a region, a tendency to develop new industries appears. This tendency to variety is often very marked, either because the best sites for the main industry are sometimes quickly exhausted, or because the main industry itself is not susceptible of growth—or, at least, on account of the competition of other areas, of growth in this region. Under these circumstances it may prove to be the case that the wealth of the region does not increase so rapidly as the population, and that the new industries owe their prosperity to a wage which, relatively to that obtainable elsewhere, shows a falling tendency. But insistence upon the same relative wage may prove disastrous to the people concerned. The area extending from Birmingham to Wolverhampton flourished at one time relatively to the rest of the country. With the growth of international trade and depletion of ore supply the position of leadership was lost and the area threatened to become derelict. Other industries were created to absorb the growing population, but some of these derived their economic strength from the fact that labour was cheaper here than elsewhere. At the same time this illusory strength was liable to be sapped by efforts to compete with foreign rivals, or better-situated rivals even in this country. Hence there was a tendency to create one trade after another. The 'natural poverty' of a district fostered a keen, alert class of business men, always ready to start new industries and to enjoy the advantages which an early start conferred. Hence the Birmingham district contains probably a greater variety of unrelated industries than any other region, and is consequently not so strongly affected by alternating periods of expansion and contraction of trade. The Clyde district, on the other hand, depends mainly upon the heavy engineering and shipbuilding trades. These are liable to extreme fluctuations, and any great disturbance in these trades produces strong and quick reactions upon the great variety of auxiliary trades, and, indeed, upon the whole local community.

It has been said that localisation is conditioned by transport facilities. The growth of shipping has led to division of labour between this and other countries. Without ocean transport we should have required to fend for ourselves, but since the advent of the steamship and the regular service which it secures the tendency to specialisation has grown ever more pronounced and the population for which the nation can adequately provide has increased without interruption.

Some nations have imposed barriers upon foreign trade, and at one time the policy of protecting home industries was pursued by ourselves. But for half a century before the war the doctrine of freedom was rigorously applied in foreign as well as in home trade. The principle that the force of competition would secure the best distribution of industry as between one region and another within the nation, and produce the greatest result in goods and services, was held to be equally applicable when nations were substituted for regions. Having had a long start in machine production the industry of the nation advanced by leaps and bounds. Manufactured goods were exported in payment for raw materials and agricultural products. Important industries, such as cotton manufacture and the metal trades, came to depend largely upon export as they overleapt the requirements of the home market. Britain became the workshop of the world, and its agriculture dwindled. As time went on, Germany and the United States fostered the growth of industries which were once the monopoly of this nation. These two countries became keen and eventually highly successful competitors in our home as well as our foreign markets, and the corresponding British industries began in some cases to show signs of decay. Those industries, such as engineering, the manufacture of iron and steel and some steel products, spelter and other minor metals, proved to be highly important during the war, so much so that there is strong reason to believe that the competition of the Germans was not of a purely commercial character, but formed part of the political policy of their rulers. It is significant that in the main German competition was precisely in those industries which have been described as 'key' and 'essential' industries—that is, industries necessary to the conduct of a modern war, or industries essential to such 'key' industries.

Whether or not Germany deliberately set out to destroy certain of our essential industries, three observations may confidently be made. The first is that the economic policy of Germany was definitely subordinated to a political end, and was so designed as to make her strong for and during war. The second is that our economic policy was based upon the assumption that the peace of nations would not be disturbed. The risk of war, or at least of such a war as would endanger the life of the community, was regarded as negligible. A militarist policy would not have been a free trade policy. Militarism, though by no means identical with economic protectionism (witness the United States) leads inevitably to such protectionism. The third observation is that the question of protecting key and essential industries is entirely a political question. If war is not a remote contingency, but a serious risk to be provided against, the meaning of the term 'economic strength' must be coloured by the fact. If, however, we are to assume that the danger of a further war is so slight that we may again legislate on the assumption that peace will not be disturbed, the term 'essential industries' loses its significance; for it refers to industries essential for war. The contribution of economics to the discussion of this branch of future economic policy is therefore essentially subordinate. The report of Lord Balfour of Burleigh's Committee was a magnificent irrelevance. It ignored the one important issue, which is whether another war is likely to occur in the measurable future. Given the same qualities in our manufacturers as are possessed by their rivals in Germany and the United States, there appears to be no reason why most of the products regarded as 'essential' should not be manufactured as cheaply as they were imported from abroad, due allowance being made for the changes produced by the war in the purchasing power of money. We fell behind our competitors mainly for two reasons. The first was lack of enterprise and an indifference to the value of industrial research, or at least unwillingness to apply the results of research. An examination of the methods employed in a large proportion of factories would bear out that statement. It is, of course, true that our industries, being older, were hampered by the existence of old plants and antiquated methods of production, while our German and American competitors were able to erect new plants which embodied the results of industrial research. But the initial advantage of the Germans and Americans disappeared as soon as they found it necessary to scrap their own methods and machinery in favour of still more recent discoveries. There is no reason to doubt that our manufacturers showed far greater reluctance than their foreign rivals to modernise their plant, or to adapt it to new requirements. The recent history of the spelter and iron trades reflects no credit upon the enterprise of the British manufacturer.

The second cause of our comparative failure in essential industries is the fact of our superiority in others. This was so marked that the effects of the failure were lost sight of in the general prosperity of the nation. The cotton, coal and shipbuilding industries flourished at the expense of agriculture and certain branches of the metallurgical industries. If in future it is decided to devote a greater proportion of our labour force to the latter our imports will diminish, and, other things being equal, the relative position of our export trades will be prejudiced. It does not necessarily follow that these will actually be smaller than in the past, for the nature and extent of foreign trade in the future will also depend upon other factors, some of which were brought into play by the war. But it does mean that exports will not be required to pay for goods which are no longer imported. It will generally be agreed, however, that a small addition to, or substraction from, the nation's income of goods and commercial services is of slight significance in comparison with the moral and political issues at stake.

2. Interdependence and Economic Responsibility

To say that regions have specialised in particular forms of economic activity and that nations have co-operated in production is but another way of saying that every region and most nations have ceased to be self-supporting. Specialised or co-operative production means interdependence, and the growth of organic unity. The modern industrial world is now a single economic entity. A serious disturbance in one part reacts upon all other parts. In spite, however, of the degree to which each nation depends for its economic existence upon other nations, none has yet explicitly recognised that opportunity to provide economic service carries with it an obligation to serve. Under peace conditions there has hitherto been no national admission of economic responsibility. The United States might prevent a corner in wheat in the interests of its own citizens : it has done nothing to prevent the exploitation of the foreign consumer. Nor do we, under normal conditions, compel exporters to provide, say, Italy with coal merely because her industries have been built largely upon a foundation of British coal. International economic responsibility and control were creations of the war, and may not survive the abnormal conditions created by the war.

Absence of any sense of moral obligation to provide economic service is characteristic not only of nations in their dealings with each other, but also of home industries in their mutual relations. The shipbuilding industry could not be carried on without ship and boiler plates, for which shipbuilders rely upon steel manufacturers. Yet these have never explicitly admitted their obligation to provide such plates in adequate supply. On the contrary, success in competition is built largely upon relative scarcity, and as the steel manufacturers, like most other people, aim primarily at making a profit, their policy will be to create those conditions which make for greatest as necessary in the public interest. But the danger of anti-social action by a monopolistic combination of workpeople is equally great. If gas and electricity were available alternatives in all houses, factories, streets and public buildings, a combination of electrical workers would be unable to act strongly against the interests of the community. But if it attempted to increase its power by incorporating the gas workers, and the attempt were successful, it would become a strong monopoly able to hold the community to ransom.

This problem is likely to prove one of the most important and difficult which democracy will be called upon to solve in the near future. One of the most striking examples of essential industries—in the present sense—is coal mining. Not inherently monopolistic on the employers' side, it is perhaps the most highly competitive of all modern industries. If a comparatively small proportion of the mines closed down for a time, no serious injury to the community would follow. But the simultaneous closing down of all the mines would soon bring nearly all forms of activity to a standstill and cause serious hardship. The workpeople have formed a strongly monopolistic combination known as the Miners' Federation, which explicitly recognises no obligation to provide continuous service. On the contrary, it emphasises not only its right to strike, but also its right to strike on any question. This may concern the members as miners, or workers employed in other industries. The point in dispute may even be a political question affecting miners and other workers, not as workers, but as citizens. This potent monopoly has become a still more powerful instrument by alliance with the railway and transport workers' associations. The triple alliance is, in fact, the strongest monopolistic combination which has yet been created in this country.

Monopolistic combinations are not, however, confined to labour. They appeared in the world of capital, before the war, not only in Germany and America, but even in this country. And one of the most marked effects of the war itself has been to hasten development in this direction.

3. The Movement towards Monopoly

In the early days of machine production the factory was still a very small affair, with a normal output which would cause men to smile nowadays. Consequently a relatively large number of factories was required to supply the needs of a given market ; and a feature of most trades was that which still remains a characteristic of the cotton industry, namely, keen competition among a large number of relatively small business units. Employers were then what, for the most part, they are now—not philanthropists, but business men engaged in the task of making a living, and as generous a living as possible. There are two ways in which profits on a given amount of capital may be increased : one is by raising the price of the unit product, the other by reducing its cost. In a stable market price can only be raised by co-operative action on the part of the producers. But in those days, when the virtues of competition were extolled, not only had most manufacturers not been ' educated ' to the possibilities of such joint action, but, even if the desire and knowledge were there, the competitors were frequently too numerous to provide any guarantee of successful co-operation.

It remained, therefore, to enlarge the surplus by reducing costs Competition was frequently so keen as to provide a strong motive to such effort. It was often, indeed, a compelling force to ensure the permanence of any surplus. A reduction in cost could be effected in either of two ways: by a reduction in wages and the prices of raw materials, the method of conducting the business remaining the same, or by the introduction of more efficient methods of production and of buying and selling. By the first method, there is obviously a limit to the amount by which costs can be reduced. But it may be taken for granted that this method was not neglected by the average manufacturer, who, in those days, had heard few if any sermons on the fallacy of the doctrine that low relative wages necessarily mean cheap labour and low costs. Employers further sought to increase their profits by constant improvements in organisation and in commercial methods. Progress in this direction meant growth in the size of the business unit, and such growth, particularly among industries engaged in making standardised products, was continuous throughout the century. Specialisation for the sake of standardisation inevitably followed, and led, in its turn, to further growth in the unit. Thus the nature of the competition gradually changed. From being fairly keen competition among a comparatively large number of small units, it became keener competition among a smaller number of comparatively large units. With the development of cheap and rapid transport, and the linking up of many areas, interlocal and finally international competition became more and yet more effective as knowledge of markets and their possibilities was more and more widely diffused. The spread of this knowledge also made it more difficult, on the whole, for individual competitors to secure any marked advantage in the markets for raw materials and the finished products.

The opening of exchanges, such as the Liverpool Cotton Exchange and the Birmingham Metal Exchange, together with the publication of trade journals, made it comparatively easy for sellers to discover what the market would bear and for buyers to learn how much or how little it was necessary to pay. The organisation of commerce in this way tended to reduce the limits between which the realised prices for a given quality varied at any given time. It operated on the whole in favour of the smaller and financially weaker firms.

The next stage in commercial evolution was the endeavour to eliminate the influence of merchants or middlemen, from whom the manufacturing firms purchased materials, and to whom they sold the finished product. Manufacturers began to sell directly and under long contracts to consumers, and to employ agents who kept in touch with such consumers or, in foreign countries, with wholesale dealers. Moreover, they entered into 'covering contracts' with firms supplying raw materials to ensure supplies sufficient to enable them to fulfil their own manufacturing contracts. In some industries the contract of a firm for its chief raw material was sufficient to maintain the contractor's establishment in employment for a considerable part of the year, and it was therefore only natural that the contract relations should grow into something much closer, and finally into actual amalgamation. To take one example, based upon recent events. A shipbuilding firm requires a large and continuous supply of ship and boiler plates and other materials made in a steel works. If these are supplied regularly, under contract, by the same steel makers, it is natural that the two firms should ultimately merge. There are obvious advantages to be derived from this course. In the first place, it makes for stability and

'official quotation' for shares shall be permitted there shall be a minimum issue of about £30,000 and a provision that "at least two-thirds of that capital shall be *bona fide* offered to and taken up by the public." [1]

There are therefore four classes of business enterprises—the public company, the private registered company, the private partnership and the enterprise conducted by an individual employer. The 'personality' of the last two is bound up with the personality of the owners, but the first two are legal entities with an existence distinct from that of the shareholders, who may withdraw without interfering with the continuity of the employing entity. The economic importance of the public company tends to grow as industry becomes more standardised and the business unit increases in size.

A business enterprise has to be promoted or initiated, and organised to meet future requirements. Capital must be collected from various sources; the type of organisation must be determined; labour must be secured and a connection with consumers established. This is no easy task. A manufacturing business should start with a reasonable expectation of a long and prosperous life and a growing output. It is therefore necessary to determine whether a particular industry is likely to fulfil such expectation, and, if so, for what form and rate of development provision should be made. It is here, in the first place, that enterprise finds scope.

Capital is provided by a judicious admixture of offers to investors. Those who seek fully secured permanent investments will prefer debentures, which are, in essence, a mortgage on the property of the

[1] Dicksee, *Business Organisation.*

company, and therefore command a relatively low rate of interest. Those in whom caution is diluted with something of the speculative element will select 'preferred' stock at a considerably higher rate of interest. This interest is the first charge on realised profits, but, unlike debenture interest, it is payable only if and when profits are earned. 'Cumulative preference' stocks stand midway between these, as arrears of interest, if any, over a period of years, must be paid, when prosperity returns, before dividends are declared. Those who prefer speculative investments will become ordinary shareholders, entitled to the rest of the divisible profits. Shareholders thus bear the risks of the undertaking, and the average rate of dividend paid on ordinary shares is therefore considerable higher than the average rate of interest paid on preferred stock, which, in turn, is higher than the average rate paid on debentures. But in a representative undertaking there is clearly a definite actuarial relation among all three, for a considerable advance in the average relative rate paid on ordinary shares would induce stockholders to substitute shares for stocks. This action would tend to raise the prices of shares—thus reducing the net rate upon the investment—and to depress the price of secured stocks—thus raising the net rate.

For the reason that shareholders bear the risks of the enterprise they also assume ultimate responsibility for its control. As it is manifestly impossible for the conduct of the business to be carried on in general meeting, the shareholders delegate control to a Board of Directors, retaining only certain powers of dealing with the most fundamental questions. But the members of the Board are so much better acquainted with the details of the business that their influence in determining even problems of fundamental policy is almost unlimited. The success of a business thus depends mainly upon the quality of the Board, and to but a negligible extent upon the shareholders. The Board of Directors—the Cabinet of the Capitalist Parliament—is thus mainly responsible for organising the enterprise, and generally contains men of different types of experience and training. One is likely to be a lawyer, another well known in the world of finance. There is now a strong and healthy tendency to include a qualified accountant. The managing director is the 'focussing point' or integrating factor of the control. He is the supreme executive officer whose function it is to carry out the general policy of the Board. Moreover, he suggests and largely influences that policy. He controls and unifies the commercial and 'productive' functions, which, however, in manufacturing industry he delegates as far as possible to 'commercial' and 'works' managers. The works manager is responsible for the internal organisation of the factory, and he may be assisted by a technical manager, and, possibly, a labour manager. But the tendency to delegate the control of labour is not yet very marked. The technical manager (or works superintendent or departmental manager) is assisted by foremen, who in turn immediately control the wage-earners. The staff organisation thus tends to become more and more complex, and the necessity for delegating functions and the importance of efficient integration become more pronounced. An ideal managing director would be an expert in legal, commercial and technical matters, a statesman in handling questions of general policy, and an able administrator capable of dealing with the human factor in industry. But whereas the need for delegating technical functions to experts has been recognised for many years, the importance of the labour problem and the desirability of delegating the work of dealing with that problem have received scant recognition. It must always be difficult to separate the labour from the technical problem sufficiently to justify their delegation along different lines, and it is impossible to separate them completely. But two points in this connection call for observation. The first is that in the public company there is a lack of any adequate substitute for the close personal intimacy which exists—or is said to exist—in small establishments owned and controlled by an individual employer or private partnership. The 'employer' of two thousand workmen is to them but the shadow of fleeting shareholders as they cross the curtain of membership. It is not, of course, simply a matter of ownership. It is largely—and, rightly understood, mainly—a matter of size. A private employer of two thousand workmen would be equally remote from his employees. The old personal relationship between employer and worker can exist only in a small enterprise. But the type of ownership itself produces a marked psychological effect upon the workmen As employees of a company they feel, in the first place, that they are working for shareholders—perhaps idle shareholders—who have only a monetary, and often temporary, interest in the establishment, and its inhabitants. In the second place, they feel that the shareholders themselves are 'functionless,' because they make no personal effort in carrying on the business from which they obtain their dividends.

The second point is that the real buffer is the foreman. Foremen, in general, are neither better nor worse than other people, but their task is the most thankless of any. It consists mainly in seeing that the men work, and work hard, when there is frequently no immediate and direct incentive to work beyond that provided by the sense of moral obligation. When men in engineering establishments (where the difficulty is most acute) are on time-work the foreman is sometimes selected not on grounds of technical knowledge, but on account of the driving force of his personality, his most pronounced characteristic being his bullying methods.[1] Many, perhaps most, managers would reply that the workmen may appeal to them or to their immediate subordinates against any arbitrary action by that type of foreman. But such power of appeal is not of much value. In the first place, men do not want to make frequent appeals against their superiors. They sometimes prefer, indeed, to allow unpleasant incidents to multiply and then to take drastic concerted action. In the second place, a man who frequently appeals against a foreman, though never without justification, comes to be regarded by the managers as a discontented workman. He may be selected for dismissal in times of depression, and, at the least, will probably become the object of further pinpricks on the part of the foreman. Again, it is believed by the men that, in the interests of discipline, if for no other reason, the manager will side with and support the decision of the foreman except in the most flagrant cases. For several decisions against a foreman would necessitate his resignation, which the firm might desire to avoid at all costs. Finally, it is char-

[1] Men on piece-work, where they respond to the stimulus, do not suffer from the bullying of foremen, because the immediate interests of the two sides are identical, and both desire an expert foreman able to remove obstacles in the way of output and to introduce improvements. The foreman is also frequently the rate-fixer, and the trouble in piece-work shops is due as a rule to disagreements regarding the appropriate rates to be paid for specific jobs.

acteristic of this country that the heads of organisations are, in practice, as inaccessible as they are said to be accessible in America. A large business enterprise is like the headquarters of a Government department, where the ordinary official's chief function seems to be to place obstacles in the way of access to the superior officers, and where the men at the centre read the tenth condensation of an elaborate memorandum written by the subordinate officer at the periphery.

There appears therefore to be an urgent need in large establishments—where the difficulty is most pronounced—for the appointment of a labour manager. By this is meant not a labour officer, holding a very subordinate position, to whom is delegated merely the responsibility of administering in the factory the laws relating to health insurance, and compensation for accidents ; but an official enjoying the same status as the technical manager—that is, immediately subordinate to the managing director or general manager, and directly responsible for general labour policy. He would represent the firm to the employees. He would be, if not the Labour Minister, with a seat in the Cabinet, at least a permanent secretary of the Ministry, responsible to the Minister for executive functions, and, through him, able to influence the policy of the Cabinet. As a specialist he would be able to devote more attention to questions of the second degree of importance (so apt to achieve the first degree) than an over-worked general manager can give, and would be able to register the lessons of experience, now so often and so quickly forgotten. Development in this direction, where it has taken place, appears to have had beneficial results. If they are to give of their best workmen must not only be fairly treated : they must also be conscious of fair treatment. A labour policy which is worth introducing and operating is worth explaining, and explaining frequently. It is worth submitting to the test of exhaustive discussion by experts who are also specialists in that sphere. The feeling that an undertaking is under the arbitrary control of an autocrat rather than working upon principles consistently applied would thus tend to disappear.

It has been stated that the shareholders bear the risks of the business enterprise. Industry is dynamic, and the movement is not uniformly progressive. There are good years and bad years, years of high prices and of low prices, periods of overtime and high wages, and of unemployment and low wages. One would naturally expect to find these alternations faithfully mirrored in the dividends paid to shareholders. But such is not usually the case, for several reasons. First, a period of prosperity and expansion is usually a period of high costs, partly on account of the high prices of materials, and partly on account of extravagance. Small economies are neglected, and much money lost that might be saved. New machinery is introduced and extensions are made. The new developments, more efficient than the old, should ensure a fall in cost. But they do not immediately fructify. By the time they are in full working order the boom may be over and the depression in full swing. But now cheapness in the methods of production counts for much, and tends to mitigate the 'evil' of low prices. Further, the firm now insists upon other economies which were disregarded when profits were easily made, and is able to purchase material at more favourable prices. Consequently, the variations in the profits realised by a manufacturing business tend to be considerably less violent than those experienced in prices or employment.

But it is important to observe that the profits actually earned in any year do not coincide with the profits declared for division among the shareholders. "Every one knows that by means of different kinds of reserves—some disclosed, some hidden—practically all permanent businesses deliberately average up their disclosed profits from time to time, because they know perfectly well that they will be expected to pay more or less uniform dividends."[1]

The policy of averaging dividends suggests that a steady, rather than a highly fluctuating return, is preferred not only by speculative shareholders, but also by business connections, who regard it as an index of financial stability. It is clear, however, that this policy can only be pursued so long as profits show no marked trend in either direction. If there is a continuous downward trend, reserves will be depleted and ultimately exhausted, and the dividends will show the real state of affairs. Under such circumstances, or if for some reason the enterprise has been over-capitalised (as may occur through a large reorganisation of the plant at an unfavourable time) the capital may be 'written down,' that is, £100 of stock may be called, say, £80, so that a given total dividend may be expressed as a rate approximating closely to the rates paid in other undertakings. If on the other hand, profits show a marked trend upwards, resulting in an unwieldy, if not dangerous, increase in reserves, or in the swelling of dividends to such an extent as to excite public comment, capital is 'written up'—that is, bonus shares are issued to such an amount as to secure that the total dividends will not be expressed in so high a rate. When bonus shares representing the capital value of 'excess'

[1] Dicksee, *Business Organisation.*

profits are issued, the stock is said to be diluted or 'watered.' It is no longer adequately represented by the tangible assets of the firm, even when allowance is made for the cost of any plant which may have proved a useless speculation. It does not necessarily follow, however, that stock is 'watered' in all cases in which bonus shares are distributed. Frequently a firm sets aside reserves which are drawn upon to finance extensions. The nominal capital remains unchanged, but the real capital, that is, the tangible assets of the firm (with an allowance for unsuccessful experiment), is increased. The capital is provided out of the 'savings' of the shareholders. The dividends are declared on nominal capital, and may therefore be considerably in excess of the rate on actual capital, though they are less than they would be in the absence of the reserve set aside for development of this character. It is a legitimate proceeding, therefore, for such a firm to issue and distribute among shareholders bonus shares representing the value of the extensions financed from the reserve fund plus the value of such reserve itself. Such action does not constitute the 'watering' or diluting of capital. It is thus extremely difficult to estimate the working results of an undertaking without an examination of its internal accounts. And it should further be observed that if the declared dividend represented the actual profits earned during any year, and the nominal capital accurately measured the real capital of the undertaking, the *rate* of dividend would not be a true reflection of profits. For a portion of the capital would be supplied in the form of debenture or preferred stock, carrying a fixed rate of interest, and the greater this proportion, the smaller the proportion of share capital, and therefore the greater the *rate* of dividend upon such capital which a given total sum would represent.

All these facts react upon the general feeling of the wage-earner. He fixes attention not on the total amount of profits, but on the *rate* paid on share capital without inquiry into the proportion which that bears to the whole, or which the nominal bears to the real capital. He sees that this rate appears to be more secure than his wages, and feels that he alone bears the incidence of depression. He sometimes believes that large sums are put to reserve, and somehow find their way—without prejudice to the ordinary dividends—to the pockets of the shareholders. He generally refuses to see in the writing up of capital anything other than the 'watering' of capital for the purpose of disguising the real position of the undertaking. He finds it difficult to believe that capital is ever written down.

The remedy for this state of affairs is publicity. Competition has hitherto been based largely on secrecy—secrecy as to the method of conducting a business, and secrecy as to the results. This secrecy affects the workers injuriously, and, as will be shown later, the community also. The workers witness the astonishing prosperity of some undertakings, and have but little opportunity, owing to the inadequate picture supplied by financial statements, of examining the losses of others.

2. Speculation and Insurance

All business undertakings are more or less speculative—that is, they involve a certain amount of risk. Plant must be laid down long in advance of demand, and preparations are made on the expectation that the demand, when it arises, will continue for a long period, if it does not steadily increase. But in the meantime—through the discovery of a more suitable alternative or by reason of a change of fashion in a capricious community—the need for the particular article may have diminished or disappeared. Or again the firm may have under-estimated the number of rivals to be taken into account, and may ultimately discover that, although the requirements of the community are no less than expected, its own share of the trade is small and precarious. One of the greatest risks of any business—or profession—is the appearance of a stronger rival.

Nothing in business is a certainty, yet all firms seek to achieve the ideal of certainty of success. They eliminate avoidable risks in various ways. A manufacturing firm requires a continuous supply of raw material which may be a natural product obtainable only at certain seasons. It must either purchase in advance and store adequate supplies or enter into a contract with a dealer for a continuous supply. The latter method is usually adopted, as the function of purchasing intermittent supplies for future use is one that requires specialised training. The elaborate market organisation of the textile and produce trades merely represents the method of unloading market risks upon specialist dealers, whose operations are based upon knowledge and foresight greater than those which could be acquired by manufacturing firms without similar and probably much more costly specialisation on the commercial side, and risk is thus reduced by being transferred to and concentrated upon experts.

The action of dealers, which is in essence "buying cheap and selling dear," tends to stabilise prices and industrial enterprise. Provided such dealers genuinely compete and their actions are based upon adequate knowledge, prices tend to vary only within the limits indicated by interest charges, for the period of 'storage,' upon the capital or value of the stored material. But in practice competition does not always work in that beneficial manner; for although the competitive force is strong the knowledge may not be adequate. Supplies may depend upon the harvest, which is 'estimated' long in advance: sometimes so long that the estimate becomes a mere gamble, bringing fortunes to the lucky.

Legitimate speculation is not a gamble, but is based upon probability. And the more constant the forces in operation, and the greater the knowledge of these, the greater the degree of probability and the less pronounced the element of gambling in the transaction. A dealer knows almost exactly the requirements in wheat of the nation. In purchasing after the harvest for sale before the next harvest he is performing a function which is necessary and will remain so under any form of economic control. He purchases a specific supply at a time when it is not wanted and sells at the time when it is wanted, thus checking a fall in prices already low and an advance in prices already high. His action thus makes for uniformity; and uniformity is worth paying for. But speculation based upon inadequate information is a gamble, tending towards instability. Its effect is disturbing, not soothing.

Contracts with dealers do not differ in essence from covering contracts with manufacturers where the 'raw material' is already partly manufactured; from the interlocking of capital or complete amalgamation—vertical integration—in the manner described in the second chapter. Amalgamation is a method of reducing risks and strengthening the firm as a competitor in its own industry; and of increasing the trade risks incurred by its rivals. But there are many risks which are common to all enterprises and which cannot be seriously if at all affected by personal efficiency or the individual action of firms. To meet these risks common action is taken. More correctly stated, action is taken by a specialist undertaking which is of service to all alike. The service is that of insurance. Insurance societies are speculators in risks, whose own 'business' risk is of a different character, and reduced to a minimum.

Insurance is rendered necessary by uncertainty: it is made possible by the "constancy of great numbers." Uncertainty is less in a group than in the individual cases comprising a group. We cannot say whether or when a particular house will take fire, but we can calculate, with sufficient accuracy for the purpose, how many houses in the country will be so destoyed in any given year. The death-rate in a community, under normal conditions, is fairly constant. And it is this group regularity of action or occurrence that distinguishes insurance from gambling, which is based upon irregularity and eliminated by regularity of action. Insurance is possible where an average varies but little, or where an appreciable degree of variation can be accurately measured. The purpose of insurance is not to prevent loss, but to distribute its consequences among a large number, thus incidentally changing their character. A destructive fire would mean ruin to an individual firm which had to bear the loss without assistance: if such losses have been insured against, they mean a regular but relatively small charge upon the business of every insured party.

The direct material loss to society is not, however, reduced.

Insurance is confined to accidents which are beyond the control of the parties and therefore "permit of an equitable contract." Insurance against fire is common: but no compensation would be paid in a case of arson. It is those risks for which it is in no way responsible that a firm provides against by means of insurance—fire, loss at sea, boiler explosions, burglary, accidents; death of debtor, partner, manager or other important individuals; dishonesty on the part of an employee ('fidelity insurance'); war, etc. These are all insurable risks, and the sphere of such risks is steadily growing larger. Insurance is thus an industry which has assumed considerable dimensions in the national economy, and one in which the 'business unit' is necessarily large and the tendency towards unification strongly marked. A large society is generally regarded as more stable than a small one for the simple reason that the risk average is likely to be more constant. The great aim of a society is to avoid concentration of risk. A municipal society whose 'ware' is fire insurance would itself be wiped out by a fire which destroyed the city. Where risks are regarded as too highly concentrated, societies adopt the system of reinsurance, by which they reinsure the concentrated risks with other societies whose liabilities lie elsewhere. This secures a form of unification which is highly desirable in the interests of security. At the same time, it preserves elasticity and fosters competition. Of recent years insurance has made the greatest advance in the social sphere. Health and unemployment insurance has been provided under the direct control of the State, and the further ex-

who wished to borrow, provided, first, that they could give ample security, and, secondly, that the loan was not likely to be of long duration—for the depositors *might* withdraw unexpectedly large sums. The loans were made at interest, which provided a profit to the goldsmith. This profit varied with the loans, and consequently the temptation to lend was—and still is—strong; and the possible loans depended upon the deposits of the timid owners of wealth. The goldsmiths, of whom there were many, naturally began to compete for such deposits by reducing the fee which they charged for providing safe custody, and ultimately paying a fee or interest for the privilege. The wealthy depositors were of course aware of the use to which their cash was put—doubtless there were occasions on which they were glad of it, and themselves obtained temporary accommodation—but so long as the goldsmith was strong enough to meet his obligations they were not concerned with the source of that strength. They might have said to him: "If you can pay me, I don't want my money; but if you can't, I do." The goldsmith was himself a wealthy man whose capital was invested in the business; and he was not likely to court loss and insolvency by lending too freely. This fact was regarded as neutralising the temptation to do so created by the endeavour to make a profit. These opposing 'pulls' are still exerted on the modern banker.

When the depositor handed cash to the goldsmith for safe deposit he naturally received a receipt for that amount—say £1000. If he drew out £100 the receipt had to be destroyed, and another written. This was an awkward method: why not give a large number of receipts for small sums, which could be destroyed as the specified sums were withdrawn?

And immediately a further step became obvious. Since the sum withdrawn would be paid to a creditor who might in turn redeposit it with the goldsmith, why not a general (instead of specific or inscribed or personal) receipt which could be handed to the creditor without disturbing the goldsmith? Thus 'general receipts' (or bank-notes) began to circulate and were readily accepted by those who knew the goldsmith and had faith in his ability and willingness to pay. These 'receipts' represented claims upon the goldsmith (now banker) for the amounts specified thereon. Nor was the next stage obscure. When the receipts were depersonalised and standardised in the form of bank-notes, and changed hands from day to day, they could not command interest and so became unsuitable for cash depositors who were desirous of leaving their money with the goldsmith at interest. These were given a deposit book (a sort of book for specific receipts) upon which was entered the amount deposited from time to time, or withdrawn, in the form of cash or bank-notes.

The transition from gold to receipts or bank-notes was easy in the case of borrowers, who thus received claims upon the goldsmith (now bank) rather than cash; and these claims or notes circulated, being accepted as substitutes for the gold. And, just as the first safe proved sufficient to meet the recurring demands of the cash depositors, so too the contents of the second safe proved adequate to meet the request for gold resulting from loans (in the form of notes) of much greater amount. The amounts standing to the credit of customers in deposit books added to the bank-notes (*i.e.* promises to pay on demand) represented the total liabilities of the bank; and these were far in excess of the total cash in the safes. The borrowers repaid their loans in time, and these sums were lent again to other—or the same—people who required accommodation. If all loans were called in and fully repaid, the cash assets would be once more equal to the liabilities. Thus, provided the securities were adequate, and the bank were given time to recall all the loans, or realise the securities, all claims could be met. The bank was not insolvent.

But frequently the bank was not given sufficient time to do this. Reference has already been made to the danger that banks might lend too freely in order to increase their profits. A century and more ago, when industrial communities in this country were comparatively small and remote from each other, they were served mainly by local banks whose credit frequently did not extend far beyond the local community. These banks sometimes lent too freely, that is, over-issued notes—for loans were made in the form of notes. The borrowers, having a new supply of purchasing power, bought goods freely and sought labour to work them up. Thus wages and prices tended to rise, and interlocal trade was stimulated. But it was one-sided trade: people from beyond the community sent goods to the profitable market, but local manufacturers, on account of their high prices, found difficulty in disposing of their own goods outside the community. The distant manufacturers had no knowledge of, and therefore no faith in, the local bank-notes. These had first to be cashed at the bank, whose gold reserve was thus depleted, and ultimately exhausted. But before exhaustion was reached the suspicion of holders of notes would be excited, and a rush would be made on the bank by all who had claims upon it. This sudden and simultaneous demand for payment frequently forced the bank to put up its shutters. Given time, a bank can discharge all its obligations; yet, from the nature of its work, it can never discharge all its obligations at any given time, without notice. The lesson of experience was translated into law by the Bank Act of 1844, which restricted the issue of notes.

But the Act quickly lost its importance through the growing use of a substitute for the note. This was the cheque. Instead of lending purchasing power to borrowers in the form of gold or notes which circulated freely, the bank credited such borrowers with the required amount against which the latter drew cheques in payment of debt. Provided no one draws a cheque which will be dishonoured, there is no essential difference between it and the bank-note. Just as the note represents an obligation to pay the holder, so too does a cheque represent a claim upon the bank; just as a note ultimately returns to the bank either in cancellation of a debt or to be deposited as cash or for exchange into gold, so too the cheque. But a cheque does not pass from hand to hand. Normally it is passed into the bank and a new one drawn to finance the second and each of the subsequent series of transactions. And, just as a bank may lend too freely in the form of notes, so too it may lend too freely in the form of amounts credited to the borrowers against which cheques may be drawn. Speaking generally, an adequate reserve of gold must be maintained to meet the bank's liabilities.

What proportion the reserves should bear to liabilities depends upon a number of factors. It is sufficient at this stage to point out that it depends mainly upon the psychology of the people, which, in turn, depends upon their education in the use of the credit system. If the community has faith in the banking method, fostered by long use of cheques and strengthened by careful management of the banks in the past, a lower reserve would be adequate than would be safe in a community which has not yet acquired such faith. In other words, so long as the people think the reserves are adequate, then they are adequate ; as soon as the people begin to fear that they are too low, then they are, in fact, too low. The purpose of a gold reserve is to maintain confidence, and so long as confidence depends upon the relative size of the reserve, the appropriate relative size must be maintained.

It has been stated that, from the very nature of its function, no bank could meet all its liabilities if called upon to do so simultaneously and without notice, although every bank which has insisted upon adequate security for loans is ultimately solvent. In view of the danger of a large call by cash depositors, banks do not lock up their money in the form of long loans. They lend for short periods (or hold secure investments which can be quickly realised) ; and they so arrange their loans that they mature and are repaid in steady rotation, so that merely by ceasing to make fresh loans they quickly cease to have borrowers. A very important form of loan—for it is essentially a loan—is that of discounting bills. For our present purpose it is sufficient to regard bills as post-dated promissory notes guaranteed by firms in whom the banks have confidence, and known as 'accepting houses.' A second important form is a short loan to 'discount houses' or 'bill brokers' who specialise in the work of discounting bills—that is, purchasing bills at their 'present' or discounted value. For example, a boot manufacturer sells boots to a dealer, who may not be able to pay his account until the boots are resold to customers. As the manufacturer may require the money immediately to pay for a supply of leather, the dealer gives him a promissory note (endorsed by a well-known 'accepting house' or the dealer's banker) dated a month hence, and the manufacturer discounts the bill at the bank or bill-broking house, and so secures funds to pay for the leather. By the end of the month, *i.e.* when the bill falls due, the dealer will have sold the boots and so placed himself in funds to meet the bill, presented by the holder to the accepting house (or bank), which in turn receives the cash from the dealer.[1]

Two important facts emerge from the above statement. The first is that bank loans are mainly used to finance trade—that is, to provide or supplement 'circulating' or commercial capital. A bank would rarely lend capital to a manufacturer to erect a new plant, for such capital would be locked up for too long a period, and might lose much of its value through inefficient management or for some other reason. Capital required for such a purpose represents a long investment and should be provided by real investors in the form of stocks or shares, or by the owner or owners of the enterprise, or by a mortgage in the case of an individual enterprise or private partnership. But the bank may safely finance commercial transactions, or provide relatively small overdrafts. In the second place, the obvious method of checking borrowings or discounts is by raising the rate of dis-

[1] Being concerned with essential function rather than machinery, I have thought it desirable, in order to state the essentials briefly and clearly, not to describe the kind of bill of exchange actually employed in business.

count, *i.e.* the charge made for a loan. The only alternative is to select the borrowers, an invidious task, even if the bankers had all the necessary materials for forming a judgment. Hence the variations which take place in the rate charged for accommodation of various kinds. If the reserves are high and the amount of loanable capital is large, the banker offers inducements to 'buyers' by lowering the price, just as a fruiterer reduces the price of strawberries in the presence of a plentiful supply; if reserves are low and loanable capital is 'scarce,' the banker puts up the price, just as a trade union forces a rise in wages when there is a scarcity of a particular kind of labour. Those who can pay the highest price are presumably those who are able to make the most profitable use of the commodity.

The first effect of the war was to destroy confidence, and the whole banking organisation threatened to collapse.[1] Hence the Moratorium, which in effect prevented those who had claims upon banks from endeavouring to realise their claims until the banks had been given time to realise their assets by calling in loans and collecting maturing claims, in the form of bills, a large proportion of which represented debts from foreigners. It has been said that the Government, by declaring a Moratorium, merely saved the 'capitalists.' It did more than that: it saved the nation. If the financial organisation had actually collapsed, no group would have suffered more seriously than industrial wage-earners. Whether the Moratorium was the only—or indeed the best—method of saving the financial structure is an open question.

[1] The effects of the war on banks and the part played by British banks in financing foreign trade are described in the writer's *Economics of War and Conquest.*

There are adverse critics : but it is easy to be wise after the event. Perhaps it is not too much to say that no act of the Government during the war was quite so successful as the declaration of the Moratorium, which paved the way to subsequent financial and industrial measures.

It has been said that insurance is made possible by that constancy of great numbers which eliminates group risks. It is the same regularity of group action that makes banking possible, and the maintenance of reserves far below the total liabilities of the bank easy and safe. The larger the group the greater the steadiness of its action. It is not surprising, therefore, that small banks tended to amalgamate, and that the amalgamations showed greater stability than did most of the constituents when they operated separately. Nor can it be denied that the English system of depositing part of the reserves with the Bank of England—thus making the banks cash depositors with the central institution—has been a source of considerable economy and strength. Not only has it tended to strengthen confidence in the banking system as a whole and, by adding to the constancy of action, reduced the total reserves necessary to maintain such confidence, but it has facilitated the financing of foreign trade and fostered the sense of responsibility of the banks for the welfare of their customers. And this sense of moral obligation has proved a stronger safeguard in this country than did the imposition, in the United States, of a legal minimum reserve.

The amalgamation or concentration movement in British banking has been accelerated by the war to such an extent that, as in the case of manufacturing industry, we are said to be witnessing the growth of a huge trust, which may strangle enterprise. But a money trust, if it came into being, would present real differences from a monopoly in manufacturing industry. A bank could not refuse cash deposits; it would also need to provide accommodation in order to secure a fund for paying interest on deposits. The extent to which it could accommodate customers would depend upon its reserves, *i.e.* ultimately, upon the amount of its cash deposits.

The amount of accommodation which would be accepted would in turn depend upon the fee charged, *i.e.* the rate of discount. The publication of the rate of discount would prevent the charging of different rates for similar accommodations upon similar securities. The danger in manufacture is that a monopolistic combination would limit output and charge different prices, according to the squeezable capacity of the market. The chief danger in the case of a banking trust would be that of providing too much accommodation, *i.e.* the over-supply of credit or inflation of currency. It is feared, of course, that a trust would discriminate against certain firms without adequate cause; but that danger could be avoided partly by Government supervision and the establishment of an independent court of appeal, and partly by a system of adequate devolution of responsibility and control.

When a customer deposits superfluous cash at his bank the currency of the country is *pro tanto* reduced or contracted. If the bank lends that sum to a customer the currency is restored to its former dimensions. Loans by a bank expand the currency in so far as such loans are actually utilised in business or otherwise. If they lie idle they do not affect the amount of currency; but loans are contracted for use.

If the loans are of such amount as to make the total liabilities of the banks dangerously large relatively to the reserves, the currency is said to be 'inflated' in the strict sense of the term. But 'inflated currency' is now loosely employed in the wider sense of expanded currency.

Expansion of currency, as we know from the experience of the last five years, raises prices during the process of expansion. The sequence is fairly obvious. Currency represents purchasing power. The possession of currency enables the possessor to enter the market for goods or services. The distribution of currency represents the distribution of the 'pulls' upon this market. If the owner does not exercise the 'pull' his currency is 'dead,' and is only revived when it is again employed. When a bank creates a loan it creates currency. If the loan merely represents the cash previously deposited, it brings the total currency back to the level at which it stood before the cash was deposited. If it exceeds that amount, the excess is created out of nothing. The total currency has been increased. The pull over the market which the borrower has acquired is greater than that surrendered by the depositor, *i.e.* his demand for goods and services is stronger: the total demand on the market shows a net increase, and, if this is large, prices rise.

The effect upon prices is precisely the same whether the expansion of currency be due to an increase of gold coin in circulation, bank-notes, Government notes, or bank credits. So long as it represents a net increase it tends to raise prices, and the period of expansion is a period of brisk trade, though not necessarily healthy trade. When the process has come to an end, the prices tend once more to become stable, at a higher level, the extent of the climb being represented by, or representing, the degree of expansion. Since, therefore, wages, employment, prices and currency are all intimately connected, no student of the labour problem can afford to ignore the currency problem.

CHAPTER IV

LABOUR ORGANISATION

1. TRADE UNION STRUCTURE AND FUNCTION

IT has already been stated that the interests of employers and workmen became divergent when extensive division of labour within a trade or group of trades began to make itself felt. This development resulted in a marked increase in the number of workmen relatively to masters, and consequently a distinct class of life-long wage-earners came into being. It has been said, too, that the real impulse and opportunity to form workmen's combinations appeared with the factory system, which brought large numbers to work behind the same works gates and made many such groups near neighbours. Without pausing to summarise the admirable *History of Trade Unionism*, by Mr. and Mrs. Sidney Webb, it may briefly be said that in the main the earlier trade unions were local organisations of separate crafts. As the country shrank with the development of railways, the local craft organisations were frequently either amalgamated or loosely federated. Many such organisations were formed during the period when the combination laws were in operation and wage-protecting associations were illegal. They were created as friendly societies, and even after the repressive laws were abolished, in 1824, and they became mainly wage associations, they continued to pay friendly benefits. The double function has survived to this day, although the position of the union in its capacity of friendly society was modified by the National Health Insurance Act of 1911.

A craft organisation is based upon the skilled occupation of the worker, not upon the industry in which he is employed. An industry such as engineering, shipbuilding or building covers many crafts, and therefore contains many unions. Moreover, a single craft, such as engineering or building, penetrates into many industries. Thus a single employer may be called upon to negotiate with many unions, and a single craft union may have separate agreements with employers in many industries. The craft unions themselves vary in character. Some, like the sheet-metal workers' and stone-masons' societies, cover one craft only, while others, of which the Amalgamated Society of Engineers is the notable example, cover a group of allied crafts, in this case turners and fitters together with (among others) pattern-makers and smiths, whose training and work differ intrinsically from those of skilled engineers. But practically all are, or were, confined to skilled workers.

In most industries in which skilled craftsmen are employed, there are large numbers of unskilled or non-specialised workers, who may move from one industry to another; and these were ignored by the craft societies. Moreover, there are industries, such as spelter and copper manufacture, in which the crafts do not predominate, and others where the great majority of the workers require little or no skill. Until the London dockers' strike of 1889 these groups and industries were more or less unorganised, but at that time a wave of unionism passed over the country and a number of unions of 'general workers' were formed. These were mutually competitive, and during the last few years their number has been largely reduced by amalgamations. Some started in single industries, such as gas works, others among special classes of workers, such as dockers and warehousemen, or municipal employees, but they gradually extended their sphere of control. The craft unions, although frequently very strong, were rarely complete monopolies. In some of the smaller towns, for example, the skilled engineers, comparatively few in number, were for long unorganised, and they tended in some cases to join the general workers' unions, to which the majority of their fellow-workers, in other spheres, already belonged. Such unions, therefore, were, and are, not only mutually competitive, but also in competition with some of the craft unions. Further, when some of the work of the craftsmen (such as moulders) was standardised and performed by mechanical aids, it was simplified and brought within the capacity of semi-skilled men, who either formed special unions or joined the general workers' unions.

A skilled craftsman generally serves an apprenticeship, and in some trades afterwards spends some time as an 'improver.' When a fully-fledged tradesman or journeyman he receives the standard rate. He may never advance beyond that rate. He stands, as it were, upon a platform or plateau in which there are but slight undulations. He cannot transfer to another craft in the same industry. The gulf between the engineer and the coach-builder in the motor-car industry is wide and deep. But the engineer may transfer to a machine-tool shop or the coach-builder to a cabinet-maker's establishment. There are other forms of industrial work which present different features, the chief being that progress from one kind of work to another is possible and general. Thus a young man in a steel works may start as a general labourer at the furnaces and expect in due course to become a fourth or third hand, and ultimately the melter. At the mills he may hope to become a roller. Consequently the process workers in such establishments are joined together by a bond which does not exist between the crafts. Nor are the interrelations of the men on different rungs of the ladder similar to those of, say, carpenters and wood-cutting machinists; for in the latter case machinery has created a new trade which is not in any sense a preparation for the skilled craft. The process workers in the 'ladder' trades—that is, trades in which there is upward mobility, though little or none between industries—naturally belong to the same association. In some industries, again, the tendency is not to link up all within a craft, or all process workers, but to form one union for the whole industry. Thus the Miners' Federation includes all the men employed in and about the mines, with the exception of small groups of craftsmen such as winding engine-men, etc. The National Union of Railwaymen includes all men employed on the railways (though not in railway shops, where the craft unions are naturally strong), with the exception of a small group forming a rival union.

It is clear even from this bald summary that the situation in the field of labour is very complex. Workers seek to form groups of people with common interests. The craft union rests upon the belief that a small closely-knit association is bound ultimately to be stronger than a larger, looser association covering groups whose interests are or may be in conflict upon important points. It is the result of the search for an organisation of people whose interests are identical upon *all* important matters. There are specific or temporary interests shared in common with the members of other groups ; and these are secured by the formation of joint committees (as in engineering and shipbuilding) for negotiating changes in standard rates.

The industrial union represents a reaction against this conception, and is based upon the assumption that all the workers employed in the various crafts within an industry have one interest in common which transcends the interest of craft. For example, it is assumed that the interest of an engineer employed on marine engines is closer to that of a plater or ship-carpenter (because all three are employed in, and their fortunes determined by the fortunes of, the shipbuilding industry) than to that of an engineer doing almost identical work in a distant electrical engineering establishment. Consequently all three should belong to the same (industrial) union, the common interests of the engineers in the shipbuilding and electrical trades being secured by a looser form of federation. Industrial unionism is also naturally advocated by those who aim at the reorganisation of the control of industry.

The purpose of a union is to safeguard the interests of its members. Its main activity is thus centred in the wages question. Associations of one kind or another are not merely desirable : they are inevitable if industry on a large scale is to be effectively carried on. Just as a wise employer favours a collective bargain with his men so, too, a wise trade union favours a collective bargain with employers ; and the formation of employers' associations is the natural reply to the formation of trade unions. The two associations appoint representatives to meet in joint committee to settle wages contracts. Such committees, varying in composition and function, exist in most of the important trades of this country, and have done admirable work. Some boards have written constitutions, which strictly define and limit their function ; others have no such constitution.

A board may have two types of questions to consider : those dealing with the preparation of a new agreement, and those dealing with the interpretation of an existing agreement. Questions of interpretation are largely mechanical, sometimes purely arithmetical, and are or may easily be referred to officials or subcommittees, and failing agreement by these, to arbitration. If the question at issue is of the nature of an entirely new bargain, or the consideration of a new principle, it is not one that either side would willingly submit to arbitration. There is no agreed standard of justice to which appeal may be made by an arbitrator, since the standard itself is the question in dispute. If no agreement is arrived at there is danger of strike or lock-out, according to which side makes the claim. If, for example, a rise in the cost of living were made the basis of a claim for an advance in wages, the employers might reply that their own industry was unprofitable at the moment. Here two different principles are at issue, and an arbitrator would not be able to give an award without pronouncing in favour of one or of a combination of the two—that is, he would be imposing some definite standard of justice upon the industry.

If the question in dispute were relatively unimportant, the two sides would probably agree to arbitration, but, under normal circumstances, they might prefer to allow a major issue to be decided by a trial of strength. This does not necessarily mean an actual strike or lock-out. Before the war the contending parties were able to gauge fairly accurately their relative strengths, and would frequently arrive at an agreement representing fairly closely the probable issue of any struggle. It is not unlikely that an important contributory cause of actual strikes, as distinguished from friction, since the Armistice is the fact that nearly five years of control have diminished the ability of each side to gauge the real strength of the other, so that they face each other like strangers and seek to test each other's real power, and the extent to which the State will permit its employment. Provided there is a definite agreement between the parties regarding the principles upon which wages should be determined, and so long as this agreement exists, the power to strike or lock-out may be surrendered and provision made for reference to arbitration upon all matters within the sphere governed by those principles. Thus, for example, the constitution of a joint committee in the iron and steel trades established for carrying out sliding scale arrangements may provide that all disputes relating to the application of those arrangements shall be referred to arbitration. But if the sliding scale arrangements became themselves subject of dispute, the provision would no longer operate. Labour has always insisted upon the recognition of the right to strike. And it should be observed that in practice, if not in theory, a strike is something more than mere withdrawal of labour. It represents an attempt to prevent the industry from being carried on during the absence of the strikers. It represents active, not passive, resistance.

The aim of a trade union is to secure those conditions of employment which it regards as just in a given set of circumstances. The most important canon of justice is equal pay for equal work, without discrimination against any individual or group. To secure this end it enters into agreements extending over a period of time and setting up standard rates of wages for specific operations or occupations. Such rates represent minima, not maxima, and are based upon the capacity and circumstances of the average man. Workers of more than average efficiency may be rated above the standard, with the approval of the union, and, on the principle of equal pay for equal work, should be so rated. Agreements of this character, provided they are faithfully observed, confer a triple benefit. That which accrues to the worker becomes evident from what has already been said. Employers benefit directly by the removal of any serious fluctuation in labour cost during the tenure of the agreement. The resulting stability enables them to enter into contracts for future delivery with greater confidence and to fix prices for such contracts with greater assurance. Long agreements are of the nature of insurance and reduce the element of uncertainty in enterprise. A standard rate, moreover, enables the enterprising firm to introduce improvements, confident that his less progressive rivals will not be able to destroy the advantage merely by reducing the wages of their own men and the labour cost of their product. It thus makes for progress and invention, and compels the laggards to press forward. Provided competition is effective, the two advantages ultimately redound to the benefit of consumers in the form of lower costs and prices.

It has been assumed that agreements are faithfully observed. But breaches, though still the exception, do sometimes occur. A trade union is not a legal entity which enters, on behalf of its members, into an agreement enforceable at law. A contract of employment is still an individual contract between a firm and its employee, John Smith or William Brown. It may cover a month, as in the tinplate industry, or an hour, as in engineering before the war. The collective agreement merely sets forth the terms upon which the individual contract should be based. Its sanction is not legal but moral. If workmen break the agreement they are not necessarily guilty of a breach of law. But it should not be assumed that only workpeople break wage agreements. There is such a thing as observing the strict letter while breaking the spirit of an agreement. Collective wage agreements are necessarily general in character. In the past they were frequently ambiguous or their sentences elliptical. They often provided ample opportunity for evasion by unscrupulous employers. Recent events have shown that the danger of interpretations which, while strictly legal, exhibit a sad spirit, is not yet over; and that the need for care in framing agreements and appointing broad-minded interpretation committees is as urgent to-day as ever in the past. Experience in State control of wages during the war shows that general agreements, be they ever so explicit, give rise to great difficulties when applied to varying local conditions, and that a generous mind is more valuable than legal training in eliciting their real intention. There is no room for the merely clever lawyer in wage negotiations.

2. Trade Union Customs and Restrictions

It has been stated that the wages ideal is equal pay for equal work, the rate being that regarded as just in the given set of circumstances. If the ideal is to be translated into practice it must be by collective bargaining; that is, the workers must be strongly organised. The association must be truly representative of the workers as a whole. If it represents only a comparatively small proportion employed in a competitive industry its agreement may soon cease to be effective even in respect of its own members. The policy of a union is therefore directed to developing its own strength. First and foremost, it must be strong—strong enough to enforce its own conception of justice upon the industry: and if the means necessary to secure and maintain this end are not in the interests of the community as a whole, so much the worse for the community. A trade union, like a trust, aims at monopolistic control, and pursues that policy which favours and strengthens monopoly. Not only so, but it aims at scarcity. Capitalistic monopolies are not philanthropic institutions: they seek first their own interest, and hope that other things will follow. But there are cases in which their own interests dictate plenty rather than scarcity. The interests of a labour monopoly always dictate scarcity. For it is not the total wages of the group that count, but wages per head. In a monopoly of capital what counts is not net profits per unit of output but net profits per unit of capital, which, at their maximum, may mean low profits per unit of product upon a large turnover of goods, rather than a high rate of profits upon a small turnover.

To say that a trade union aims at monopoly is not to imply criticism. The justification rests upon the alternative and the use made of monopoly. The mere fact of monopoly suggests advantages and dangers—possibilities rather than realities.

The importance attached to collective bargaining provides the real explanation of the value placed by the craft unions upon the customs and restrictions which accumulated during the nineteenth century.

Perhaps the most important of these is apprenticeship. For the efficient pursuit of a skilled craft a fairly long period of apprenticeship is essential, and is insisted upon by most craft unions. The system is a survival of the old days of domestic handicrafts. But it is more than that. It is a method of regulating entry into a trade and limiting the number of its members. The emphasis is laid not upon training but upon control. Where possible and desirable, even the number of apprentices is limited. And where the conditions are such that control can only be secured by abandoning or relaxing apprenticeship regulations, they are not allowed to stand in the way. Thus engineers and compositors have been compelled, by the sheer necessity of controlling their trades, to accept as members those who were taught by other systems than that of apprenticeship. Regulation of entry into a trade is thus a method of securing and preserving monopolistic control, collective bargaining and the standard rate. But when it proves a hindrance rather than a help it is abandoned, and with it provision for adequate training.

Closely connected with apprenticeship is the custom of claiming certain kinds of work as the monopoly of the skilléd craftsman. The official attitude towards the introduction of new machinery and the simplification of processes is not to-day one of antagonism: but the union may prevent the operation of a simplified machine or process by a semi-skilled worker. Sheet-metal working, for example, is a skilled craft in which machinery is still in its infancy. It consists of a group of operations many of which, taken separately, are semi-skilled or unskilled. But the organisations either oppose sub-division of work or alternately, claim the separate semi-skilled operations for their own members. The aim of this policy is to strengthen the monopoly by maintaining as large a field of work as possible for the group of craftsmen already in that field.

The demarcation difficulties in shipbuilding and other trades are explained in the same way. The 'natural' boundary line between two crafts may not be clear and straight, but faint and crooked. In some cases there may be no dividing line and it becomes necessary to draw a more or less arbitrary one. Each of the crafts naturally desires to make its own field as large as possible. Encroachments by other crafts are deeply resented, because they reduce the field of immediate employment to those attacked, and so lessen their power of controlling the conditions of employment. If fitters or bricklayers do more, there is less for plumbers or masons to do. On the other hand, if the boundary line is clearly marked no craftsman will cross it, for two reasons. The first is the loyalty of craft to craft, the second the fact that the wage, if determined by output, represents specific payment for specific work, and any extension of work is in effect a reduction of piece-rates.

The attitude of workmen towards machinery and output is governed by the same consideration. While their associations objected to new processes they defended their action on the ground that the resulting increase in product from a given number of men reduced the demand for labour and created unemployment. The official opposition to new machinery has practically disappeared, and official bodies are mainly concerned with the conditions under which it shall be introduced. As already pointed out, they generally claim the work for their own members as long as it is possible to do so. But there remains a considerable amount of unofficial and local opposition to new processes, and the general attitude of the rank and file of workers remains suspicious. What they fear is not so much a general decrease in the demand for labour as an immediate fall in the demand for that kind of labour for which machinery has been substituted.

For the same reason strong objection is frequently taken to unrestricted output and schemes for stimulating production. Restriction as an official policy has been abandoned, but it was nevertheless practised before the war. The general attitude towards methods of remuneration will be examined more fully in the next section, but it is relevant to the point we are now discussing that many engineering and shipbuilding workmen object to payment by results on the ground that the increased production per head thereby secured reduces the number of people required in the occupation affected.

In general, trade union and 'unofficial' customs fall into three categories. First, there are those which are intrinsically good and point the way to legislation. The insistence upon a standard minimum has been justified by results, and the principle has since been endorsed by Government both in the Trade Boards Act and in wages legislation during the war. The strong instinctive dislike to overtime which in some cases had become almost normal is thoroughly healthy, provided it does not result in cast-iron regulations against overtime. Even regulation of output may, under certain conditions, be desirable. In the heavy chain industry the employers found it necessary, in the interest of output over a long period, to establish a 'stint,' representing the amount of work per day which the chain-maker should produce. Previously the latter had responded too fully to the immediate stimulus provided by payment by results, and his output was uneven, and on the average less than the stint. The mile cannot be done at a sprint.

The second group of customs represents mere survivals of a bygone age, when the methods of production were wholly different. They are restrictions in the full sense of the term, and can no longer be justified. They exist in many industries, but as they are generally local and unofficial they do not admit of illustration. The third group represents those defensive measures designed to meet specific dangers, justified in some circumstances, but superfluous, even anti-social, in others. The primary object of the apprenticeship regulation, as enforced by craft unions, was not to secure a supply of adequately trained labour but to control numbers and prevent undercutting by unqualified workers. When it failed of its object it was abandoned or relaxed. Nevertheless an important secondary result was that it did secure training, and until some adequate substitute is found it will continue to justify its existence. The control of numbers was necessary to preserve intact any agreement with employers regarding wages and general conditions of employment. The report (1913) of the Industrial Council on industrial agreements suggests that this end could be secured by legislative action. In effect it recommends that any agreement arrived at between associations of masters and men covering a substantial majority of the workers of any trade shall be applied by law to the whole trade. This seems a wise recommendation and was adopted in principle in the Munitions of War Amendment Act, 1917, and the Wages (Temporary Regulation) Act, 1919.

Action of this kind would render some restrictions superfluous. But it would need to be accompanied by a measure to secure adequate training of a sufficient supply of labour in the skilled trades. Apprenticeship should be regarded as a branch of education, and such facilities provided as would make it possible for any boy, however poor, to benefit by it. Hitherto the cost of apprenticeship has been so great and the immediate profitableness of blind-alley occupations relatively so large that the skilled workers have tended to become a 'close' group, like professional men and employers, with a truly professional indifference to the fate of those outside their circle. Equality of opportunity, if it is to be real, will mean less onerous financial conditions of apprenticeship; but it will also mean more searching tests of efficiency. It is not that skilled crafts will be less difficult to enter, but the nature of the difficulty of entry will change. At present there are no real tests—none on the road to check the inefficients—and the training itself is mechanical, partial and otherwise unsatisfactory. A really scientific solution of the problem will contain even more than this. It will provide an organisation not merely, like employment exchanges, for indicating the actual and registered needs of industry, but also for estimating its requirements in the future and affording guidance to the bodies responsible for training and advising youths seeking careers in the most promising fields.

If the prejudice of workers—in all grades—against improvements in methods and unrestricted output is to be overcome provision must be made for those who may be forced to fall out by the way. Such provision will be twofold. It will offer insurance against unemployment, and a scheme for the automatic selection of those who are to be dismissed. It is clear that a journeyman at the height of his powers, with, perhaps, a growing family to provide for, should not be selected as against a youth with no social responsibilities and young enough to train quickly for another post, or ' mobile ' enough to go to another part of the country, or as against an elderly man on the point of qualifying for an old-age pension. This difficulty is reduced by the legal guarantee which would be given to the standard rate, making it impossible for an employer to retain an old man at a low rate in preference to a younger man at the standard rate. But it will still remain a difficulty, for although the employer may desire to dismiss the least efficient at the standard rates, such a policy may not always be in the best interests of society. Insurance against unemployment of this character is obviously desirable ; and a general insurance scheme offers advantages over one integral to any one industry which might be completely revolutionised by the new methods. In any case the fact that crafts cut across industries, and that most industries are always in a state of flux, separated by boundary lines either arbitrary or constantly changing, would render the narrower scheme impracticable. Moreover, the wider and more general scheme, covering as it does a larger group, stabilises the average rate of dismissal. Industries, in respect of methods of production, move in jerks, and an average for purposes of insurance would not only vary widely between various industries, but be very difficult to discover for any one of them.

Any insurance scheme of this kind would require to be closely linked up with the training scheme, so that apprentices, disappointed in their expectations, might immediately be offered facilities for training for alternative employments.

The insurance scheme should cover not only those displaced by new machinery and improved organisation, but also those thrown out of work by trade depressions. It is frequently urged by workmen—particularly engineers and shipbuilders—that one result of increased output under piece-work is over-production and depression of trade. Whether this view be true or false—and it seems to be mainly false—periodic depression and unemployment for which the worker is in no way responsible is a fact of industry. Unemployment insurance is therefore not merely desirable but, by providing income during the period of idleness, would tend to check the spread of industrial depression and accelerate recovery from it. Insurance and training would thus render superfluous certain restrictions which would otherwise remain necessary in the interests of the crafts.

3. Methods of Remuneration

Industrial efficiency depends largely upon the spirit of the workshop. Without the hearty co-operation of the workers the most powerful mechanical appliances and the most efficient organisation are of no avail. One of the more serious errors of many who advocate 'scientific management' is to believe that men can be parcelled out like bales of cotton, the appropriate muscles being employed in the most 'economical' manner without reference to the volition of their owners. But the first step in management which is really scientific is to enlist the co-operation of the worker and to trust to his sense of 'sportsmanship,' which is never completely absent, and which, in most of the relatively few cases in which it is weak, can be fostered and developed. The spirit of the workshop depends partly upon the method of remuneration and the conditions under which it is introduced. That some craft unions still attach supreme importance to method of payment, as distinguished from amount of weekly earnings, is evident from the antagonism which has been evinced during the past year to payment by results on highly standardised wood-work in aircraft factories.

The attitude of trade unions towards methods of remuneration will only be understood so long as it is borne in mind that the unions aim, above all things, at the maintenance of the standard rate, and believe that this can only be achieved by collective bargaining. Consequently no policy which militates against collective bargaining can be expected to meet with their approval.

Wages represent payment for work done. Provided therefore the results of such work are measurable, individual payment by individual result is the natural or obvious method of remuneration: it secures the closest approximation to 'equal pay for equal work,' which is an ideal accepted on both sides. Differences arise mainly in the translation of that ideal into practice. In some cases, such as agricultural work, retail distribution and teaching, the result of effort—in which quality may be an important factor—cannot be measured with that accuracy which is necessary for the purpose of payment by results, and the workers are therefore paid according to time, the desired correlation of work and pay being secured, as far as possible, by supervision or inspection. In other cases, such as steel manufacture, or the rolling of sheets or plates, the product can be easily measured, and the quality checked ; and piece-work (either uniform and individual as in sheet steel rolling, or collective as in brass and copper rolling) secures the desired equality of payment, and is not merely readily accepted but strongly pressed for by the workpeople. In yet other cases, such as coal-mining, supervision is extremely difficult, and an incentive to work must be provided in the form of payment by results, even where the system may be in other respects relatively unsatisfactory.

Uniform piece or tonnage rates, if they are to secure equality of payment, presuppose, first, that the result varies directly and solely with the efforts of the workers and, secondly, that the objective conditions under which the men work are uniform and unvarying.

At blast furnaces the output depends partly upon the men, but also partly upon factors beyond their control, such as the quality of the material, the size and character of the furnace, the nature of the blast, etc. The present method of payment is thus a compromise between time and piece-work—namely, a datal or time basis rate to which is added a (tonnage) bonus on output. It is interesting to observe that so far from defending the day-rate and objecting to the output bonus (as engineers do) the workers at blast furnaces appear to be strongly in favour of ' straight tonnage rates,' which would vary from furnace to furnace, as the bonus does at present, but which could be fixed by negotiation between the two associations. The method would be consistent with collective bargaining, for, first, there are few furnaces in a plant, and, secondly, once fixed and tested the rates would require but slight and infrequent modifications.

In coal-mining the objective conditions show considerable variation, and tonnage rates are reinforced by minimum time-rates to meet the requirements of abnormal places. Where conditions are standardised and fairly uniform, piece-rates are 'depersonalised' and can be fixed by collective bargaining, but the only alternative to the time minimum for work in abnormal places would be 'individual' tonnage rates, which, on account of the difficulty of measuring the degree of abnormality, would frequently be of the nature of a gamble. If the extent of abnormality could be ascertained it would be possible, even practicable, to establish machinery for applying to such circumstances principles which had previously been agreed upon by the two associations.

Such machinery exists in cotton-spinning, which is a piece-work trade. Piece-rates are fixed, by collective bargaining, for standard machinery and raw material of standard quality. If the objective conditions deviate from the normal or standard in any factory the rates are adjusted to the required amount by two assessors, full-time servants of either side. One important difference of principle is observable in the determination of rates in cotton-spinning and mining where the conditions deviate from the normal. An antiquated machine or poor material in spinning carries a rate above the standard, the excess being necessary to secure equal pay for equal effort. The same principle applies in steel manufacture. But in mining, tonnage rates in poor mines may be lower than in average mines. The difference is due to the fact that in manufacture the firm is mainly responsible for the conditions, and may escape the penalty of a high piece-rate by introducing better methods or securing better material. Thus differentiation against the unenterprising firm stimulates improvement in method and makes for industrial progress while providing justice to the men.

But the poverty of a mine is due to nature and the evil cannot be completely remedied by mechanical devices. If therefore it is to continue in operation the working costs must be reduced. The alternatives to the men are employment at lower rates and migration to other mines or districts. Hence, partly, the refusal of the Government to specify a uniform national minimum day-rate in the Coal Mines Act. Such a rate would probably have rendered 'abnormal coal mines' permanently unprofitable. It is not unlikely that one of the advantages of 'unification'—whether by nationalisation or other means [1]—would be to remove from the shoulders of the workers the burden imposed by ungenerous nature and to facilitate the closer correlation of pay and effort.

The above considerations enable us to appreciate the difficulty experienced by some of the craft unions, and to understand their reluctance to accept fully the system of payment by results. Skilled moulders generally refuse piece-work on heavy castings on account of the extreme difficulty of estimating a just piece-rate. On the north-east coast this difficulty has been partly met by the establishment of a lieu-rate, the workers being paid, say, time and quarter (there are two or three lieu-rates) in time of pressure on the understanding that they work at a 'piece-work speed' The system enjoys the great merit of being an appeal to the men's honour.

Blast furnaces and engineering works are poles apart. The latter contain a large number of machines for various operations such as turning, planing, drilling, screwing, grinding, etc. Nor are the machines for performing such operations all alike, or the methods employed identical in different shops engaged in

[1] See Chapter VII.

manufacturing similar products. No industry exhibits so great a variety of machinery or of methods of production on the same group of machines. Engineering is a group of industries among which there are great differences, and within each of which there is a great variety of form, so much so that a 'typical' engineering shop can scarcely be said to exist. There are establishments which concentrate on one product or on a small group of products, such as a machine tool shop making one type of lathe, or a fuze shop. But the majority of shops, varying enormously in size and organisation, 'specialise' in general work. In such cases therefore piece-work among skilled engineers must be mainly of a strictly 'individualised' character, differing essentially from piece-work in, say, sheet mills, where the same rates for the same processes may obtain throughout the district. It is not wholly a question of multiplicity of products. Skilled sheet-metal workers make an enormous variety of sizes and products, such as lamps, trunks, brass jugs, motor-bonnets, motor-radiators, petrol-tanks, etc. Yet in some places they are largely employed on piece-work, the union having prepared an elaborate schedule of piece-work prices which employers are requested to pay their workmen. But the products are made in large numbers, and the orders constantly repeated. In general engineering, on the other hand, the jobs not only vary from day to day but may never be repeated. If similar products are made in different shops the machines and methods employed may differ materially. The jobs often approximate, in type, to repair work, which is never twice the same task. When, therefore, a price—or what comes to the same thing, a time allowance—has to be fixed for a job it is usually done by negotiations between the rate-fixer or foreman and the individual workman or the shop steward. If by chance the job is repeated or a similar one given at a future time, the foreman, having the old schedule at hand, is at an advantage. If the old price provided a balance regarded as excessive, the new price is reduced. Again, if a series of similar products have to be made, 'experimental' piece-rates are fixed, which, if they are found to be 'excessive,' are reduced; or an exceptionally quick worker is called upon to do the experimental work, and the price is fixed in accordance with his rate of production.

The objection to piece-work is due mainly to the individualised nature of the bargain and the fear of rate-cutting. Nor is this fear without adequate foundation in the history of the past. There are, however, two kinds of rate-cutting: the one is theoretically justifiable, the other is a gross injustice. Piece-work provides a stimulus to effort, and if it is individual rather than 'group' or 'collective' piece-work, the stimulus is direct and personal, and therefore at a maximum. Earnings vary directly with personal effort. An average time-worker is paid to work, not to be idle. There is an implied assumption that he will do a fair day's work. If on transference to piece-work he is able to make double or treble his time-rate, either the piece-rates have been fixed too high, or, if they bear a close relation to labour cost when he was on day-work, he was a slacker, and has now responded to the stimulus. In either case, provided he is an *average* worker, not an exceptionally rapid worker, there is strong justification in theory for a reduction in piece-rates. There must be some definite relation (implicit or agreed upon) between the day-rate and the piece-work earnings of the *average* worker over a fairly long period, which allows for a short 'sprint.'

A wise employer will not, however, press the application of this principle too far. For he will recognise that the 'stimulus' is a delicate creature. Under favourable conditions even the supposed average worker may exhibit unsuspected qualities of workmanship, and discover 'short-cuts' which enable him to increase his production out of all proportion to his continuous effort, but which would have remained undiscovered on the time-work system. In the second place, if piece-work earnings are 'expected' to be, say, time and quarter, and the workers know (as sometimes they do know) that additional earnings would be the signal for a 'revision' of piece-rates, they are tempted to 'ca' canny' during the trial period and afterwards to limit the output to such an amount as will regularly bring them time and quarter. Under such conditions not only do the benefits of piece-work not mature, but in extreme cases the output may even be less than on day-work.

Piece-rates are sometimes cut in a manner which is grossly unjust to the average worker. This occurs when a number of workers are on similar jobs and the piece-work earnings of the most rapid workers are taken as the basis for revision. Workmen, like employers, vary tremendously in point of efficiency, and a piece-rate which does and should give the average worker a 'fair' balance may secure, in individual cases, a relatively large weekly income. It is clear therefore that the question of payment by results is one which cannot be treated lightly. Some unions oppose the system, others (like the Amalgamated Society of Engineers) adopt a neutral attitude by regarding it as an establishment question. The greater the degree of standardisation the stronger the tendency towards payment by results. But as the tendency to regard standardised or repetition work as semi-skilled is now equally strong, standardisation of itself leaves the problem of the highly skilled craftsman untouched.

Some firms have endeavoured to solve the difficulty by means of collective bonuses on output, such output being measured in product if standardised, or, if not, by invoice value. Most experiments of this nature appear to be in engineering, but the conditions during the war and since the armistice have been so abnormal that no final estimate of their value can yet be offered. Moreover, the 12½ per cent. bonus prescribed by the Ministry of Munitions in 1917 wrought great havoc among those which had already been instituted, and 'queered the pitch' for those in contemplation. But two observations—the one adverse, the other favourable—may be made upon the principle of a collective bonus. Against it is the fact which destroyed associations of producers in the nineteenth century—namely, that the share of each worker depended less upon his own efficiency than upon that of all the others. The workers thus tended to become eager superintendents of their colleagues' activities and to pay less attention to their own efforts. This tendency would be less pronounced where the product passed through a long chain of workers than where the majority were similarly employed. The favourable effect would be, in some cases, the influence which it would produce on the spirit of the establishment and the necessity it would create for the formation of a 'bonus committee' whose functions might be gradually extended until it became a fully fledged works committee animated by a really constructive purpose.

A collective bonus is usually based on invoice values

when the products are too varied to permit a bonus on specific product. But the total invoice values are determined not only by the amount produced, but also by the selling prices of the specific products. In practice therefore the bonus is a sort of half-way house between a bonus on specific output and those sliding-scale arrangements which once prevailed in coal-mining, and have survived, and even been extended, in the iron and steel trades. Under these arrangements the wages of the employees, both time and tonnage workers, vary with prices ; that is, certain day or tonnage rates and a certain price for iron or steel are taken as standard or base wages and prices, and every change in price (say 5s. per ton) is followed by a percentage change in wages. Usually it is a collective arrangement covering a group of similar firms, and the prices are the average prices received over a period of four months for the output of a selected number of the group.

Sliding scales are therefore in essence a method of distributing among a group of workpeople a share of ' excess ' profits due to a boom in trade and a rise in prices, or a share of the loss incurred during a period of depression and low prices. Where there are advances on scale, particularly where the standard wage is also a minimum, such advances represent windfalls, and, in theory, are clearly distinguished from the normal or standard rates. In principle therefore they are closely akin to profit-sharing schemes, though they differ from these in one important respect. Profit-sharing schemes are based upon actually realised net profits which, in consequence of inefficient management, may be considerably less than market prices might be expected to provide. Sliding-scale arrangements, being based on prices, eliminate the insecurity due to possible variations in the efficiency of management and provide the workpeople with a share determined by the profits which a representative firm might be expected to enjoy.

Moreover, whereas profit-sharing schemes are usually restricted to individual firms, the sliding scale usually covers a section of an industry, such section containing many firms. At first sight sliding scales restricted to individual firms appear to be fairer than those covering a group of firms, as the prices realised by the individual firm represent more accurately than a group average price the ability of the firm to pay. But the larger scheme proved to be fair on the average; it also tends to uniformity in the method of contracting for future orders and penalises inefficient management and commercial organisation, the danger of which is one of the great weaknesses of individual profit-sharing schemes.

Although sliding-scale advances are theoretically 'windfalls' to the workers, in practice they have become inextricably mixed up with standard rates. Thus, to take a striking pair of examples from the iron trade, the Cleveland blast furnace scale was first introduced in 1879, a year of extremely low prices and wages. The price and wage rates existing at that date were adopted as standards, with the result that in 1914 prices were far above the standard, and a considerable percentage advance on sliding scale was being paid, part of which would have been secured on the standard wage if there had been no sliding scale. The Lincolnshire blast furnace scale, on the other hand, was established shortly before the outbreak of war, when the prices and wage rates adopted as standards were relatively high, and in 1914 the advances on scale were of relatively small amount.

The base or standard rates in the two cases are therefore not comparable ; the equivalent of the Lincolnshire base rate in Cleveland is the base rate plus the scale advance at the date when the Lincolnshire scheme became operative. Thus part of the scale advance in Cleveland is no longer of the nature of a windfall, but a part of the normal remuneration expected by the workpeople, and comparable to the advances in standard rates gained in other trades since 1879, and due to the general increase in the cost of living.

It is clear that sliding scales are only suitable for industries the products of which are highly standardised and fairly simple. Coal-mining is such an industry, and for many years the miners were paid according to definite scales. Every coal sliding scale has been abolished, the last to disappear being the South Wales scale. Probably there were many reasons for the antipathy with which these scales were regarded by the miners, but one of the most important was the confusion of the ' windfall ' with the standard rate. "The dam'd thing has no bottom," said the men, who were not prepared any longer to share the risk of so highly speculative an industry. But even until the peace of the world was disturbed their wages did, in effect, vary mainly with the average price of coal, such price being regarded as the test of the ability of the industry to bear an advance or delay a reduction.

Although the principle of the sliding scale appeared to be sound—namely, that the wider the area of distribution of ' accidental excess profits ' the better—and is capable of extension beyond its present sphere of operation, there are many industries, such as transport, and manufacturing trades in products which vary widely in shape, size and quality, for which the sliding-scale system is obviously unsuitable. In such industries schemes whereby workers share in the realised profits have been tried by individual firms, with varying success. Most profit-sharing and co-partnership schemes either provide that the share of the individual workers shall be reinvested in the firm or merely offer capital shares to the workers on favourable terms. The aim in all such cases is to give the latter an interest in the business, and it is held that the investment of capital in the enterprise secures a greater stake in the business than is given by a simple share in profits which the men may spend as they care.

Profit-sharing schemes have not always been popular among the workers who have had experience of their operation. Complaints are made that profits practically disappear for long periods, and that, taking an average of years, the workers' share is so small as to destroy the value of the scheme. Suspicion is sometimes entertained that the amounts placed to reserve, which are not controlled by the men, are increased in order to reduce divisible profits. In any case labour has no voice in determining policy, upon which profits so largely depend. The granting of a share of profits is generally an 'act of grace' on the part of the firm, and often accompanied by onerous conditions, and terminable at will. Organised labour, for the most part, has been openly hostile to profit-sharing schemes, under which the men are dealt with individually. It is argued that most existing schemes are aimed against or offered as alternatives to trade unionism.

It may be true that these objections are based upon the practice of but a small proportion of those firms which have adopted the principle of profit-sharing. But it would be foolish to ignore the feeling of the workers and the attitude of their organisations. The first condition of success is the moral support of both workers and their chosen leaders, and to enlist such support it is necessary to construct schemes to which the workers shall be parties, not as individuals, but as groups.

The construction of such schemes, in establishments where they are desirable, may be regarded as an appropriate function of workshop committees, to which reference will be made in the seventh chapter.

CHAPTER V

THE SYSTEM BEFORE THE WAR

1. The Theory of Competition

THE complex organisation of modern economic society has been built up on the basis of economic freedom, or freedom of enterprise.[1] Every one, that is, is allowed to carve out a career for himself without interference by the State. The first condition of individual success is the provision of service to society. If all are successful, it is because all provide services for which society is willing to pay: and society is therefore provided with the services it requires most urgently. Such appears to be the broad assumption upon which the system rests. There is no conscious and deliberate co-operation of integral parts. The organisation is not controlled by any 'external' authority conscious of its own directing power, but regulated by a force within itself, the centripetal force of personal competition. Although, under peace conditions, the attitude of the State is mainly passive it cannot disclaim ultimate responsibility for the system. The State is obviously finally responsible for a system which it may destroy or strengthen. But it has hitherto refused to effect on it any radical transformation. The theory governing the attitude of the State is that the internal regulating force, with its silent persistence, is the best

[1] See Marshall, *Principles of Economics*, book i. chap. i.

that has yet been discovered for the purpose. Its action may not always and in all spheres be productive of the best results, but it is productive of the best general result. Where its action produces evil consequences these can be neutralised by specific measures. The regulating force must itself be regulated, but it should not be destroyed. Industry and people can presumably best serve the community by being left to themselves: the presumption is against interference, and the burden of proof of the need for interference rests upon those who desire it. Industry and workers, *qua* workers, are deemed to be innocent of anti-social action until found guilty upon evidence. The State asks, "Why should I interfere?" not "Why should I not interfere?" These questions, indeed, convey the essential difference between the real Individualist and the true Collectivist, who live in different hemispheres though they may sometimes meet at the Equator.

Economic freedom, which means freedom of enterprise, does not necessarily mean industrial competition. It includes freedom of contract and association, freedom on the part of firms to arrange not to compete with each other, and on the part of workers not to undersell each other's labour. It covers freedom of combination, and such combination may be monopolistic. As an operative force competition has, indeed, lost its efficacy over a wide range of industries, and threatens to lose it over a still wider range when the immediate effects of the war have disappeared. Competition, in short, accomplishes its own destruction and the creation of monopoly. In examining the value of economic freedom as the guiding principle in economic society it is therefore necessary to pay attention to the self-eliminating character of competition and the monopolistic form of control which follows upon its destruction. But, although economic freedom embraces both competition and monopoly, and the various intermediate stages between these two, it is frequently regarded as the competitive system, and the case which has generally been offered in its defence rests upon the assumption of industrial competition. Industrial competition, it is said, secures that the wants of society will be not merely supplied, but supplied, on the average, at the cost of production, that is, without the payment of 'unreasonable' or 'excess' profits. It is true that manufacturers charge 'what the market will bear,' but in a competitive market all will be compelled to charge the same prices. Where surpluses appear they are due to one or more of the following causes. First, a factory or other enterprise may be far better situated than its rivals, and the cost of collecting the materials and distributing the product considerably below the average in the industry. But the resulting surplus is ultimately either shared or entirely absorbed by the landowner in the form of higher rent or royalty, and the problem is therefore more a land problem than an industrial one. In any case the surplus should not be handed over as a gift to a small minority of consumers or special group of workers. Secondly, a trade or group of trades may enjoy a boom due to foreign demand or some new and sudden need at home, and all the rival firms, whose intercompetition is temporarily suspended, may charge prices well above cost and enjoy excess profits. But if the new demand shows any probability of permanence new competitors enter the industry, supplies are increased and prices once more fall to the cost level. In practice the temporary effects of the booms are neutralised by recurring depressions. In the third place, individual manufacturers may exhibit qualities of industrial and commercial management above the average in the trade, and enjoy excess profits which are denied the remainder. But these, like the excess profits due to a large and rapid increase in general demand, create forces which in the end destroy them. The less enterprising are ultimately forced to adopt the methods of their more enterprising rivals (*i.e.* to 'get on or get out') and the lowest cost becomes the general and price-determining cost. Such excess profits thus merely represent a temporary payment for a benefit ultimately conferred upon society in the form of lower prices. Such, baldly stated, is the case for competition among firms.[1] The prospect of excess profits is the real stimulus, but the more effective the stimulus the smaller the chance of such excess and the shorter its duration when it appears. At a relatively small and temporary gain to individuals the community enjoys a permanent and growing benefit in the form of increasing abundance and lower costs reflected in lower prices.

Nor does the system, if fully operative, act unfairly upon employees. An employer offers, and is forced to offer, sufficient wages to attract an adequate supply of labour. If he offers more he will attract too many workers : he is compelled to offer a sum representing the commercial value of the labour, for if he does not he will be enjoying excess profits which will attract to the industry rivals who will outbid him in the labour market. If therefore workpeople voluntarily distribute their labour over the industrial field in accordance with the need for such labour, the relative wages paid

[1] Excess profits due to expansion of currency is noted in Chapter VI.

in different occupations will represent those which are regarded as just by the workers themselves.

This abstract theory is nowhere accepted without serious modifications. Yet it is important that it should be stated somewhat in this form, as though competition acted 'in vacuo,' there being no economic friction. For much, if not most, industrial legislation aims at precisely that result which is said to be secured by perfect competition, and is ultimately based upon the assumption that the most serious evil in the system of economic freedom, as it actually operates, is not competition but the lack of it, and the jerky manner of its operation where it appears to be effective.

Before testing the assumptions of the optimistic competitive theory described above, it may be observed that the term wealth is used in a narrow sense, and that the balance sheet is seriously incomplete. Admitted that keen rivalry in a manufacturing trade will lead to the employment of the most efficient methods of production and the provision of the product at a correspondingly low cost, whether measured in money or in labour energy directly employed; the fact remains that the immediate interest of the consumers of this product—who may be distributed over the globe—is confined to that product: and they will naturally look at that industry from an entirely different standpoint from that taken up by the people who live in the neighbourhood of the factories, even if they do not work there. The point is not merely the conflict of interest between worker and consumer, which will be separately examined: it refers also to the social by-products of geographical concentration of industry and the local reactions of certain kinds of trades. As I write these lines in Oxford, I am deeply concerned—selfishly speaking—at the reduction in

firms may remain a secret for long periods, thus repelling firms whose entry into the trade would increase supplies and so bring prices down to cost level; on the other, workers may be ignorant of their 'commercial value' to their employers and therefore accept lower wages than they might successfully demand if their knowledge of the market were better, or without knowing it they may be wanted by other employers who would pay higher wages.

Finally, potential competitors, knowing the possibilities of the market and desiring to exploit such possibilities, may not be in a position to utilise their knowledge or give effect to their desire. They may not be trained for the kind of activity called for; they may live too far away—for man and his family and furniture, as in Adam Smith's day, are heavy baggage to transport, and inertia is a powerful force. Apart from inertia, the cost of removal may be so great as not to justify a change for a small increase of remuneration. Under peace conditions there were considerable local variations in prices and wages.

Competition, in short, assumes equality of opportunity, that is, opportunity of acquiring full knowledge and mobility between trades and professions. Such equality did not exist before the war. It is not necessary, of course, that all the members of one group should be able to move into another group: changes on the part of a small proportion would frequently secure the necessary adjustments of supply and therefore of remuneration. But even that small degree was frequently lacking. There were privileged professions and privileged skilled trades; there were industries in which the capital necessary was so large that adjustments were made but slowly, and excessive gains or serious losses ruled for considerable periods. Moreover, the 'market' is frequently a future market, and its conditions will be determined not only by the factors already indicated but also by the power of realising the future and the determination to provide for it. Such is the case particularly with wages, and its influence, together with that of the other factors, may be shown to exercise considerable influence upon the wages of the vast majority of women workers and, indeed, of all sweated workers. Much of what is stated in the next section on the subject of women's wages is also applicable to the wages of unorganised male workers employed in unskilled occupations. The section is intended to serve as an illustration of the difference between competition in practice and the optimistic competitive theory already described. The third section provides a further illustration of a somewhat different character.

2. Women's Wages before the War[1]

The problem of women's wages, like that of men's wages, has been profoundly altered by the circumstances produced by the war. According to the census of 1911 nearly six million women and girls over twelve years of age were employed as wage-earners in England and Wales alone, so that it is likely that at least six and a half millions were so employed in Great Britain. Although reliable statistics on the subject are lacking, it is commonly believed that the average wages of female workers were considerably less than one-half the average wages of male-workers. The causes of the great difference in average wages are fairly obvious. A number of occupations, such as heaving coal, filling blast furnaces, metal rolling, boiler making and repairing, shipbuilding,

[1] This section is substantially one part of a memorandum submitted to the War Cabinet Committee on women's wages.

brassfounding, etc., call for greater physical strength and endurance than the average female worker possesses, and constitute a natural monopoly to male workers. Again, a number of skilled occupations—the better known crafts such as sheet-metal working, carpentry and skilled engineering—were prohibited to women by the rules and customs of the craft unions, which controlled entry into such occupations by more or less strict apprenticeship regulations. Such action was not confined to trades, for a number of professions, such as law, accounting, etc., were equally prohibited to women. Even where the trade or profession was not explicitly denied them by regulation, it was denied, as in the case of banking, by time-honoured custom. Moreover, girls, to whom paid work but infrequently represented a life career, were generally averse from spending the time and incurring the expense necessary to prepare for skilled trades and professions (or their parents discouraged such a course), and this strengthened the custom of regarding such occupations as the monopoly of men. The fact that so large a proportion of women teachers took the short cuts to the profession, thus cutting themselves off from any chance of promotion, gives point to this statement. The capital expenditure in money and effort necessary for adequate preparation for the higher grades of professional service or for skilled manual trades could only be repaid, with interest, over a much longer period of years than that which constituted the normal expectation of working life for the female adolescent. Hence, partly, the smallness of the proportion of those women workers in clerical occupations who aimed at or had the opportunity of attaining the more responsible office posts. The unpreparedness of the average worker reacted upon the view taken by employers of the capacity of woman to undertake the higher grades of work.

Thus the avenues of employment open to women were fewer than those available to men, and these, too, were on the whole the less desirable avenues. And they resembled each other far more closely than they resembled the avenues which were closed to them by rule or custom. They were on the flatlands of industry and offered no pleasing prospects. Who could walk along one could walk along many; little or no training was necessary. It was therefore inevitable that the concentration of almost the whole supply of women upon an extremely limited range of occupations, most of them calling for no special qualifications, should result in extremely low wages, and in wages which ranged, on the whole, between narrow limits over a large proportion of those occupations. For a woman worker was a potential if not actual competitor for a considerable number of occupations open to women. A maidservant one day might be a shop assistant the next, and, later, in the Midlands, a machine operator in an engineering establishment. But the ease with which the transition could be made was a more important factor than the actual number of transferences which were periodically made.

The position of women wage-earners was further weakened by the absence, until recent years, of combinations. Even when attempts were made to form trade unions, success was limited by that mobility between trades to which reference has just been made. In a sharply defined and homogeneous industrial area such as Cradley Heath, a small region where over two thousand women were employed in chainmaking, the formation of an occupational union was relatively easy; but in a large, diverse, industrial and commercial region such as London, where the women workers are distributed over a wide range of occupations, among which there is considerable mobility, the problem of trade unionism offered almost insurmountable difficulties, at any rate until the passing of the National Insurance Act, which called for the formation of approved societies for female as well as male workers.

The evil effects of individual competition among a large supply of female workers for a restricted number of occupations were intensified by the diverse character of the workers in respect of social responsibilities. Some were in search only of pin and pocket money, and depended on the family wage-earner for the necessities of life; and to a proportion of these regularity of employment, or sixpence more or less, was not so significant as in the case of others who were themselves the family wage-earners. The heterogeneity of the competitors for work possibly led to competition of a more deadly character than that which usually prevails among equals, and was itself a factor tending to increase the difficulty of combined action, which would already have been extremely difficult if all the members had had precisely the same interests and responsibilities.

But the position of women workers had considerably improved in many occupations during the years immediately preceding the war, as was evidenced by the increasing difficulty of obtaining domestic servants, whose wages showed an abnormal increase. Thanks to the effect of education upon the imagination, initiative and enterprise of young women and girls, occupations were entered hitherto regarded as restricted to men. Old customs were rapidly breaking down and traditions disappearing. The avenues of employment were rapidly increasing in number, and women's capacity was steadily expanding. But their education was not complete, and they were frequently guided by conceptions (or misconceptions) of social status conferred by certain occupations, and therefore accepted positions, for example, in shops at considerably lower pay, in preference to, say, domestic service. And the larger and better known shops were able to command workers frequently at less favourable conditions of service and pay than smaller shops, so much did the factor of social status count in the minds of the workers.

Various explanations of the inequalities of men's and women's wages have been offered. Some, observing them to be inequalities between the sexes, have fastened upon the 'sex' explanation. Men, it is stated, are the family wage-earners: women normally require to fend for themselves only. And their needs being fewer and their expenses less than those of the family, their wages are naturally lower. Those optimists who believed the world in which they lived to be the best of all possible worlds, naturally adopted this explanation as the justification of the existing differentiation, which appeared to secure some approximation towards payment according to need.

The position calls for careful examination, more particularly as it is so widely accepted at the present time. It is probably true that the proportion of adult male workers who have dependents is greater than in the case of women, and that this difference was increased during the war, but it is also true to say that the difference in such proportion was always exaggerated in the minds of the public. For it has been stated that under peace conditions between one-half and two-thirds of women workers had others partially or wholly dependent upon their wages for sustenance.[1] The dependence of others was sometimes due to the inadequacy of the wages of the 'family wage-earner,' husband, father or brother. But the evil of low wages, as already implied, was merely intensified, not created, by the absence of dependents in the case of women who worked only for their own pecuniary advantage. Even if all such women had had dependents, their competition would have been of the same form, and, in the absence of combination, would have produced almost the same results. It has even been argued, with considerable force, that the absence of dependents strengthened the women's wages market in that those who were free from 'encumbrances' were less ready than others to surrender or abate their claims to better conditions, and had greater reserve power in the bargaining process. However that may be—and reliable evidence upon which to base any judgment is lacking—differences between men's wages and women's cannot be fully accounted for in the manner described. If all men with red hair had been subjected to the same disabilities in proportion to their numbers as women workers were, the results would have been the same, and the fact that such men were responsible for the maintenance of families would have had but a remote bearing on the case.

The explanation of the differences between men's and women's wages is of the same nature as that of the difference between the wages of skilled and unskilled adult male workers. Unskilled workers were faced with difficulties of the same character as women workers in general. And those who emphasise the social injustice of the so-called differentiation between the rates paid to men and women also emphasise,

[1] What value may be attributed to these figures I cannot say. They are not essential to the argument.

by implication, the social injustice of the differentiation between skilled and unskilled rates for men.

The reference to social injustice naturally leads to a discussion of the moral responsibility of employers of women workers. The fact that employers were able to command the services of women and girls at relatively low wages enabled them to create industries whose very existence depended upon the cheapness resulting from such low payments. The profits of the employers were not relatively large. The women were therefore paid their commercial value to the employer—that is, their wages, although low, represented the net value of the product of their labour. But it has already been stated that the variation in wages over a large field of women's activities was very small, on account of the intermobility of female labour. In this respect women differed from men, among whom the requisite intermobility was only secured by differentiating between the wages paid in different occupations. Theoretically the standard rates in any given occupation are, under competitive conditions, such as will attract the requisite supply of labour, and no more. And these naturally bear a definite relation to the standard rates in other occupations. It is true that custom impedes the action of competition, and that labour frequently regarded in abstract theory as fluid has a 'crusted surface': but that such custom and inertia merely retard or impede and do not totally destroy the force of competition in the industrial life of labour is shown by the manner in which labour responded to the call of high wages in munitions works in 1915–16 and the consequent need for comparable advances in other industries.

The marked tendency towards a norm in women's

wages meant that even in those competitive industries which could ' bear ' relatively high wages, and where perhaps men had once been employed, wages were extremely low. But even in such cases profits were generally not above the normal, if indeed they were as high. Keen competition between employers meant that the advantage was ultimately transferred to the consumers. The employers of sweated workers were in their turn frequently sweated by dealers, and the latter by consumers.[1] Thus even in such industries, under the prevailing economic conditions, the women workers were paid the commercial value, to their employers, of their work. This is partly what is meant by the economic generalisation that the worker is paid what he or she is worth.

Any discussion of the moral responsibility of the individual employer must therefore take into account his opportunity, or lack of opportunity, of effecting any improvement. Where opportunity is lacking moral responsibility does not appear. An employer who is himself a victim of the economic circumstances already described cannot be blamed for the lowness of the wages paid to his workers, except in so far as he ignores an opportunity of securing collective action on the part of himself and his competitors.

By collective action on the part of employers an improvement may in general be effected, and the incidence of the additional payments to workers passed on to buyers. A monopolistic employer is in a position similar to that of an employers' association, and therefore bears a far greater moral responsibility than an

[1] Presumptive evidence in support of this statement is contained in the balance sheets of industrial companies, which show that high wages and large profits usually appear together, and generally appear where the units of production are large.

individual employer in a highly competitive industry. But the moral obligation under pre-war conditions even of a powerful body such as an industrial combination, municipal authority or government department was extremely difficult to determine. For industries are sometimes mutually competitive in respect of products, and a large group not mutually competitive compete for female labour. And apart from the limits of power of a body controlling an industry which may not be able to 'bear' substantial advances restricted to that industry, it was frequently held that no sectional body, even a government department, should set up a highly revolutionary standard of payment. This theory held sway among public bodies and in the Government service, where the aim was merely to act as a 'good employer' without introducing highly disturbing conditions of service. The one who sets the pace is never very far in advance.

The difficulty of effecting substantial changes by a mere stroke of the pen was experienced by the Trades Boards established under the Act of 1909. These Boards, which established minimum rates in specified trades, had to work under certain objective conditions for which they were in no way responsible and which restricted their power for good. Their action was guided by so-called practical considerations; they had to act experimentally and to pay constant regard to what the 'market would bear.' The results of the Act thus proved somewhat disappointing to those ardent social reformers who looked for sweeping changes without delay. But the Boards conceived their task to be mainly to effect such improvement as was possible in the given economic organisation; not to effect great changes in that organisation.

3. Industrial Unrest before the War

Trade unions exist to settle the terms of wages contracts, and wages were regulated before the war mainly by the cost of living. The workmen in a particular trade aimed at such a rate of remuneration as would secure the standard of living regarded as 'just' for that trade, due regard being paid to the cost of preparation in early youth and the objective conditions of work. The relative rates paid in different occupations thus tended to remain constant; the actual rates rose and fell, not simultaneously, but after the same sort of struggles, and in the absence of special circumstances all with the cost of living. Industrial friction was almost inevitable during the process of adjustment; but the adjustments themselves were generally of the same nature, for the same important factors were present in all. Occasionally new trades emerged, and had to be 'placed,' or existing trades sought a higher financial status in the existing group. But the great majority of the older crafts had determined their relative positions, and most adjustments were adjustments in the actual wages of most categories of wage-earners.

It has been said that the defence of the competitive system lies in the fact that competition compels constant improvements in methods of production, which, without any fall in wages rates, reduce costs and prices. Under such conditions wage-earners, like all other consumers, would enjoy the benefits of industrial progress through the steady increase in the purchasing power of their income. Their standard of living would thus rise as the national income of goods and services per head increased.

But during the period of almost twenty years

immediately preceding the war, in spite of great concurrent technological and commercial progress, prices rose steadily, and in the absence of advances in wages rates the position of the wage-earners would have been considerably changed for the worse. In spite of those advances which were secured from time to time it seems fairly evident that the majority of wage-earners were little, if any, better off at the end of that period than at the beginning, and that they therefore enjoyed little or no benefit from the industrial progress which had been effected. The position calls for careful examination, for, in the first place, the advance in the cost of living was the most important cause of pre-war industrial unrest, and the hardening of the conviction that the competitive system had failed. In the second place, it has a strong bearing upon the problem of economic reconstruction. The interrelation of wages and prices remains one of the most important, urgent and difficult problems in the economic world.

The rise in prices during the eighteen years immediately preceding the war was due to expansion of currency, a subject to which reference has already been made in an earlier chapter. It was there shown that while currency was partly gold and partly credit, the amount of the latter which a nation could safely 'carry' at any time was closely related (in time of peace and financial freedom) to the quantity of gold. The annual average production of gold showed a rapid and fairly steady increase after 1896, due mainly to the exploitation of the African mines made possible by the discovery of the cyanide process. The new supplies, which in a few years amounted to a considerable percentage of the previously existing supply, found their way to all countries. They helped to swell the currency, which was further expanded by the credit currency issued on the new gold, and by the development of the banking system in the newer economic regions (such as the southern states of North America), which resulted in an increase in the proportion of credit currency to gold currency. Thus the total volume of currency increased even more rapidly than the supply of gold. But the new gold was the main cause of this increase. It has been said that gold is the foundation of modern economic civilisation. While the statement contains a large element of truth, it is, nevertheless, hardly too much to say that the pickaxe of the African miner was hacking at the foundation of modern political civilisation.

Without halting to examine the details of financial machinery it may briefly be stated that the gold coming to this country, and the credit currency which it propagated, meant *new* and additional purchasing power which could be transferred by the banks to traders of various kinds. These, 'armed' with the new currency, entered the market as competitors, or stronger competitors, for goods and services of various kinds, the prices of which naturally rose. If the supplies of new currency had ceased after a period—or, more correctly, had been restricted to the requirements of a growing population and an expanding economic organisation—prices would once more have become stable, but at the higher level. But the new supplies appeared year after year in excess of such requirements, and the general level of prices continued to rise, with occasional checks due to trade depression, until the outbreak of war. For reasons which cannot be stated in brief compass, retail prices rise and fall more slowly and within narrower limits than wholesale prices, and wages vary less than retail prices. An upward trend of prices reacts unfavourably, and a downward trend favourably upon wage-earners as a whole. And in this respect what is bad (or good) for labour is good (or bad) for owners of capital. The period under consideration was a period of rising prices and high rates of profits, and a period during which organised workers were endeavouring to recover by wages advances the ground lost through the fall in the purchasing power of the sovereign. The resulting industrial friction was not a phenomenon confined to this country: in greater or less degree it characterised every modern industrial community in which the workers were organised.

During the same period new countries were passing through a process of rapid economic development. Where labour was scarce wages readily responded—and more than responded—to the rise in prices. The materials for development—railway material, machinery, etc.—were obtained from the older industrial communities. Thus the rapid development of Canada during the first decade of this century was enormously facilitated, if not, indeed, made possible, by imports from this country. During that period we exported 'capital' in large amounts. Financially the statement means that people in this country invested their new wealth in the new foreign securities; industrially it means that we exported more, by that amount, than we imported. If a relatively poor man saves he deprives himself of immediate pleasures for the sake of a future gain: during the period of abstinence he is no better off (in respect of immediate pleasures based upon spending) than he would be if he cast his savings into the sea. Similarly with a nation. If a considerable proportion of its labour energy is devoted to the making of goods to be sent abroad without immediate return it forgoes the satisfaction of immediate consumption: the possible standard of living for the time being is reduced. Ultimately interest payments are made and the capital may be repaid. But during the process of exportation, capital invested abroad means sacrifice. This sacrifice is imposed in the form of higher prices, produced by the competition for goods and services on the part of those firms upon the position of which the foreign requirements have reacted. The rise in prices due to the expansion of currency was therefore accelerated and accentuated by the export of capital.

The immediate effect of expenditure on armaments in this country is precisely the same as that of the exportation of capital. Provided such armaments are simply and solely of the nature of insurance, the ultimate effects are also similar. Both represent immediate sacrifice for future gain, the material gain in the one case being the absence of material destruction caused by war, in the other the return of the capital with interest. But in practice armaments are not always of this character. In some cases they tend to create the very danger against which they are regarded as insurance, and in so far as they do this they produce a double loss, the immediate loss of goods which might have been produced by the labour devoted to armament building and the final destruction caused by the war which they produce.

It has been stated that a period of rising prices is a period of high rates of profit. Most industries flourish and large fortunes are made. It is also a period of extravagance following upon the growth of such fortunes. Expenditure upon extravagant luxuries was very marked in the early years of the present century, and produced a twofold effect, psychological and material. The spectacle of this expenditure brought the contrast between rich and poor into sharp relief. Moreover, the effect of such luxurious expenditure was to intensify the rise in prices caused by the factors already enumerated. The popular feeling was soon reflected in the writings of economists [1] who were careful to point out that the mere size of the national income was not an adequate index of welfare, and that it was necessary to examine the constituents of such income and to place the various items in different categories determined by the degree to which, in practice, they contributed to the development of the race.

The contrast between the West and the East ends of a city, between the rich and the poor, was fastened upon by those who advocated the abolition of the competitive system, and led people to seek a method of reconstituting economic society by collective effort. The labour movement became more and more political, and the new Labour party achieved considerable success in the general election of 1906. It was—and remains—a party aiming at the ultimate establishment of a collectivist State; and a considerable improvement in economic conditions was anticipated by organised labour as the result of its initial success.

The feeling of unrest, in so far as it pervaded the mass of relatively well-paid and generally skilled workers, was due to the adverse way in which they had been affected by the upward trend of prices and general trade activity. The greater regularity of employment and increased opportunity for overtime did not compensate for the reduction in the value of the sovereign. Overtime, indeed, was not always acceptable. The terms of employment are

[1] See, in particular, Clay, *Economics for the General Reader*.

laid down in agreements normally covering fairly long periods. The rates specified in such agreements represent to the workers a certain standard of living and it is assumed that during their tenure the cost of living will remain constant. If for any reason a marked change takes place the agreement appears to be obsolete and in need of revision. If it is not revised a severe strain is imposed upon the loyalty of the rank and file. During the period under consideration, when prices rose fairly rapidly, and the men suffered while their employers enjoyed, or appeared to enjoy, increasing profits, the strain sometimes proved too great, agreements were broken and unofficial strikes took place. The violation of an agreement in this way enjoyed—or suffered from—full publicity, and the general public, which heard little or nothing about those agreements—an overwhelming majority—which were faithfully observed, was encouraged to believe that a wage agreement was a mere 'scrap of paper.'

The rise in the cost of living was therefore mainly responsible not only for the pre-war industrial unrest but also for the form which it took in the few cases in which unofficial strikes occurred. There were, of course, contributory causes. The expectations raised by the election of 1906 were not realised, and a reaction against parliamentary methods was witnessed among the younger leaders in some of the most vital trades. Some of these were largely influenced by syndicalist ideas which were carried by a south wind to South Wales, and later spread to other regions. But the general strike was not a Syndicalist myth: rather was it an instrument to be employed as soon as possible and as often as might be necessary to prove—or, as others would say, to compel—the bankruptcy of the competitive system. Other young leaders turned to Marx and became revolutionary socialists. But the vast majority, too impatient to differentiate between various schools of thought and too eager for action to appreciate the importance of their differences and antagonisms, became merely revolutionary leaders remaining largely indifferent to the architectural basis of the new society. Among people predisposed to resentment they scored momentary triumphs ; but their influence before the war was negligible except in small, though important, districts. South Wales was one of these districts. Here it was reported that the profits in the coal-export trade were abnormally large, and it was known that the miners lived in deep, narrow, tree-less valleys, under housing conditions which in many cases reflect great discredit upon the nation.

The objective conditions under which people live must exercise a profound psychological influence. The manifestations of industrial unrest have been more serious among the mining valleys of Glamorgan and Monmouthshire and on the Clyde than in other parts of the country. These areas are the most fruitful breeding ground of extremists. Yet the main industries in the two regions—coal-mining in the one and engineering and shipbuilding in the other—in no way resemble each other : nor are they wholly confined to these areas. Reference has already been made to the physical characteristics of the mining district. The Clyde engineers and shipbuilders work under grey skies, in which the sun rarely shines during a long winter. When it doesn't rain it threatens to rain. When the day's work is done the workmen pass through the factory gates into streets bordered by tall, forbidding tenements—miles of them. When the sun does shine in winter its rays have no chance to reach the lower flats of the high tenements and the flats themselves are so expensive that the *majority* of the workers can hope for no more than one or two rooms and kitchen. It may be argued, in reply, that the average skilled worker, if he valued better housing conditions, could well afford to pay the rent charged for a more commodious dwelling. There is point in this criticism, to which reference will be made later. But the fact remains that the distribution of house-room in that area is such that even before the war only a negligible fraction of the wage-earners would be able to give effect to a desire to remove to better houses than are now occupied by the average worker.

Generally speaking, the period during which the trend of prices was upwards was a period of trade activity. But trade activity does not necessarily mean prosperity. A great deal depends upon the forms of activity, and these in turn depend upon the way in which wealth, in the sense of purchasing power, is distributed. But even trade received occasional checks. While the trend of prices was indicated by an ascending line, the gradient was not always the same, and there were occasional dips, such as are met with in mountaineering. The dips represented slumps of trade, either slight, as in 1901, or more pronounced, as in 1907. Nor were these slumps new phenomena. Ever since machine production was introduced they have made periodic appearances ; and when they appear they are accompanied by unemployment, and frequently by distress. Their ultimate cause is to be found in the system of divided labour and the consequent need of producing in advance of requirements. They are inevitable (though their evil consequences and present intensities are not) so long as people retain freedom of consumption, and they represent in part the difficulty of anticipating future needs. They are intensified by the difficulty of correlating producing capacities at different stages of manufacture and by the fact that manufacturers, in seeking to estimate future demands are influenced by each other. They communicate optimism and pessimism; their temperature ranges from that indicating low vitality to fever heat. The body of manufacturers are like a ship which, in a hurricane, may drag its anchor—the banking system. Periodic unemployment, against which provision is inadequate, if any exists at all, creates dissatisfaction and influences policy. Workmen prefer steady uninterrupted work and regular wages to irregular work and fluctuating remuneration. And they feel that by working overtime or responding to the stimulus of payment by results during a boom they are merely accelerating the depression and intensifying it when it appears. Their view may be wholly false—it is certainly no better than a partial truth, the part which is true being but a small fraction of the whole truth of the matter—but it has largely influenced the judgment of many employed in those trades (particularly marine engineering and shipbuilding) which are more seriously affected than others by depressions. Such depressions visit all industrial communities, whether they are borrowing or lending communities, and whether they are protected by tariff walls or protected by freedom of external trade.

Most of the causes of labour unrest already enumerated operate throughout the modern industrial world. The precise effect they produce depends largely upon the character of the people and the nature of their political institutions. The wage-earners of this country to-day are undoubtedly better off than those of two generations ago. Not only are they better fed, better clothed, even better housed, they also work under more favourable conditions. But they are also better educated, and are more keenly sensitive of their position, and more alive to the possibilities of the future. It is for this reason that the statement that the position of the wage-earner is steadily improving leaves them cold. The statement is not, of course, wholly true of the present century; but even if it were strictly true, they would reply that the rate of improvement is not so rapid as it might and should be. They are far more deeply impressed by the contrast which still exists, even if it had not become more marked, under peace conditions, between rich and poor, which they believe to be the contrast between their employers and themselves. Unlike their fathers they refuse to regard this state of things as inevitable, and what is not inevitable may be unjust. What was previously an evil thus becomes a grievance. They look upon it as the result of the competitive system, and therefore begin to question the justice of that system.

Nor is this all. Education has made some of them more keenly sensitive to the relationship implied, or believed to be implied, in the wage contract. They regard themselves not as equal parties to a contract, but, by virtue of the discipline imposed upon them in the factory by the employer, as in a position of subordination. Hence the growing use of question-begging epithets such as 'wage-slavery,' 'capitalistic domination' and the like. It is not that they necessarily object to the individual employers; their objection is rather to the system which denies, or appears to deny them the status to which, as responsible citizens, they are entitled. They regard industrial democracy as either a corollary or even an essential preliminary to political democracy; and some of them believe that the first step towards democratising industry is the abolition of the competitive system, not by gradual steps, the pace being partly determined by developments in other countries, but here and now, irrespective of material consequences.

We are not concerned at this stage with the intrinsic value of these views, which will demand attention later, but it is necessary to refer to them as factors operating in the minds of ambitious young leaders even before the outbreak of war, and partly determining the modes in which the feeling of unrest occasionally found expression. The status of the worker in industry was a more important question in the minds of not a few of the unofficial leaders than the possibility of improving their material conditions by advances in wages.

CHAPTER VI

ECONOMIC REACTIONS OF THE WAR

1. Industry and Commerce

WAR, in the purely material sense, generally results in net loss. For it means the destruction of the lives of people who might have been employed in making goods and providing services upon which the standard of living depends; the destruction of property brought into existence under peaceful conditions; the destruction of goods specially prepared for carrying on the war, and prepared by people normally employed in adding to wealth as defined in time of peace; and the employment as soldiers and sailors of citizens who previously served the ends of peace. War thus reduces the capital and income of the world. When two nations or groups of nations are at war a third may, and frequently does, gain by the conflict, just as extravagant expenditure upon dress on the part of a lady may be a source of great profit to her tailor. But the gain of the neutral is at the expense of the belligerents. A belligerent nation, moreover, may, under special though highly improbable circumstances, secure a material gain through conquest, exceeding the individual loss produced by the conflict. It is conceivable, indeed, that a war may add more to the wealth of the world than is destroyed in battle and preparation for battle.[1] It may be stated, however, without fear of contradiction, that the recent World War has resulted in an enormous economic loss to the world as a whole; and it is probably true that in spite of the unequal distribution of this loss, and temporary gains by individual nations, no important state, belligerent or neutral, was as wealthy at the end as at the beginning. Nevertheless, some of the states, even belligerent states, such as the United States of North America, suffered far less material loss than others, such as France. Their proportionate loss in men was far less; their capital remains intact, if it has not largely increased through material assistance rendered to the Allies, and they suffered less disturbance of trade. Their 'pull' upon the wealth of the world has therefore been strengthened, and they will necessarily assist the economic recovery of those states which have suffered most. In the long run, therefore, their material balance sheet may indicate a net gain. Great Britain is not in that position. To this country the war entailed a material loss which will be felt for many years to come. It is idle to pretend otherwise, and to hold out hope (as some people do) of as high a standard of living for the mass of the present generation as would have been possible if the war had not occurred. It is equally futile to pretend that early recovery even of the pre-war standard of living is possible except by serious, sustained and well-directed effort on the part of all workers, by hand and brain.

The economic existence of this nation, while its population remains at the present level, is bound up with international trade. A considerable proportion

[1] These points are discussed at length in *The Economics of War and Conquest*, by the present writer.

of the necessaries of life and of the raw materials upon which depend manufactured goods essential to the distribution of such necessaries, is obtained from foreign countries. The war seriously interfered with foreign trade, partly through loss of shipping, partly because enemy countries ceased to send goods and Allied states were unable to send in such large quantities as before, and themselves required from neutral states goods which would otherwise have found their way here. The result was shortage. And the shortage was intensified by the fact that a great proportion of our producers were withdrawn from peaceful occupations to serve in the forces, and a further large proportion to provide munitions and other essentials of war not required in time of peace. That was the basic economic fact with which the nation had and still has to reckon. The system of economic freedom, which is based upon the assumption that peace exists to facilitate the production of plenty, broke down, and the state was compelled to find an alternative. The antithesis of economic freedom, if not its only real alternative, is economic conscription, and the five years of war was a period during which there was a strong movement in this direction. The labour difficulties of the period merely marked the difficulty of establishing and maintaining the new system in various departments of economic activity, and particularly the partial failure in applying it in the sphere of prices. Roughly speaking, the first year of war represents the phase during which the system of economic freedom was tried and failed; during the next two years serious restrictions were imposed, and the ground was prepared for a far greater degree of control of all kinds in the last period of two years. The 'vigorous policy' of the Lloyd-George administration was but the natural development of that previously employed, and was only made possible by what had gone before. By the end of the war we had progressed beyond the stage intermediate between economic freedom and economic conscription, and only a few minor trades and pursuits were not regulated, directly or indirectly.

The task of the Government was twofold—to secure and distribute supplies. Supplies were obtained by production at home and purchase abroad. Their distribution involved rationing and price control, functions which were found to be inseparable under conditions of shortage. The first problem of production was to secure an adequate supply of munitions, and to this end the Ministry of Munitions was established in the summer of 1915. The primary function of the Ministry was to organise the manufacture of guns, ammunition and other essentials of war, but the performance of this function involved many other activities. It was discovered that to control the final stage of manufacture effectively it was necessary to organise the earlier stages and also trades ancillary to the main trades of engineering, shipbuilding and the manufacture of explosives. Some of these were wholly inadequate and had to be considerably enlarged, particularly iron-stone mining and quarrying, iron and steel production, spelter manufacture, the coke oven and by-product industry, etc. In spite of these efforts, supplemented as far as possible by importation from abroad, supplies remained insufficient, and the system of 'priority' or rationing according to urgency of need was introduced. In this way it was possible to conscribe all industrial effort conditioned by a supply of the controlled goods, and to secure the greatest possible economy in their use. The supply of labour was also inadequate, and it will be shown later that the principle of rationing was also adopted in this sphere. The Admiralty performed similar functions, and worked in co-operation with the Ministry of Munitions. Although the details were not precisely the same, the War Office control of the woollen trade and that of the cotton trade by the Cotton Control Board (working in close conjunction with the Board of Trade) presented essentially the same problem. Nor did those confronting the Food Production Department and the Coal Control Department differ in their fundamental conditions.

Organisations for the purchase abroad of supplies of goods not obtainable at home were also set up. The State became merchant as well as industrial producer, and the wheat and sugar commissions were early at work, and acted as intermediary between foreign sellers and wholesale dealers at home. But circumstances did not permit the importation of adequate supplies. Where there is a shortage prices, in the absence of control, are apt to rise to a degree quite out of proportion to the deficiency, and the race is to the rich. For this state of matters the simple control of prices is no remedy—it merely gives the prize to those who are first in the queue (whether it be a whisky, theatre or meat queue), and the result is as unsatisfactory as before. The corollary—indeed, the primary condition of any successful price control—is rationing. This double function was performed by the Food Control Department, the Railway Executive and the Shipping Control Department (for the shortage extended to land and ocean transport) as well as by those Departments already enumerated.

The State thus supervised the activities of private producers and itself became manufacturer where necessary ; it restricted the powers of sellers at home, and took the place of purchasers of goods from abroad. But in the foreign markets the State at first merely competed with other (foreign) purchasers, and was compelled to pay the world prices. As there was a world shortage, these were highly inflated. Neutral countries, chief of which at this time was the United States, reaped the benefit, and our Allies were our chief competitors. With the entry of the United States into the war there was a strong movement towards inter-allied economic control, the principle of price control being extended and that of rationing according to need being applied to nations as well as individuals. Thus the Allied Munitions Council was established, followed by the Inter-Allied Food Council (with its 'Programme Committees' such as the Inter-Allied Wheat Executive) and the Allied Maritime Transport Council. Under this group of organisations neutral as well as allied States were rationed. The development towards international co-operation in the economic sphere is of the first importance, for it represents the first explicit recognition of economic responsibility, and the first surrender of the right on the part of one state to exploit the necessities of another. The principle of distribution according to need was accepted without reservation. The United States exported wheat to Europe not merely out of her surplus, but out of stock required for home consumption. We exported coal to Italy at a time when it was scarce at home. It is, of course, the case that the doctrine of joint economic sacrifice was accepted under stress of war, when common sacrifices were required for victory and economic and military requirements were almost indistinguishable. Nevertheless, it is possible that it will make an epoch in the history of nations and lead to a degree of economic co-operation which, before the war, would have been regarded as an impossible ideal. There is already the prospect of international labour legislation. It is but a short step to the international control of trusts. International economic control and responsibility may have come to stay, though the precise form which it took during the war is rapidly disappearing.

Having accepted the twin principle of rationing and price control, it became necessary to determine the general level of prices to be permitted by the controlling authority. The term 'general level' is used advisedly. Under peace conditions there is a degree of mutual sympathy between prices which is not generally recognised. Where two commodities, such as tea and coffee, or beef and mutton, are complete or partial substitutes, it is well known that their prices rise and fall together so long as the methods and costs of production remain unchanged. Scarcity in one which raises its price results in an increased demand for the other with a consequent rise in price. But this sympathy, though less marked, extends beyond substitutes, and exists in respect of practically all commodities over fairly long periods provided there is no marked change in methods of production, and provided, moreover, that they are produced and distributed under competitive conditions.[1]

[1] Economists may point out that I have ignored the fact that some commodities are subject to the law of diminishing returns, and others to the law of increasing returns, and that therefore their prices, following costs, may diverge rather than move in sympathy. But the changes in prices to which I am referring are those consequent upon or appearing concurrently with expansion of currency, and *in practice* the tendency towards divergence is therefore not nearly so strong as the opposing tendency. Thus it is sufficiently near the truth to state, as I have done, that the sympathy is less marked. It may sometimes occur that the redistribution of income which is

The price controlling authority cannot altogether ignore this general relationship of individual prices without discriminating in an invidious manner between industries and occupations. This was done in the classic example of house rents. The ' price ' of shelter was controlled, and the controlled price was fixed at the pre-war level; with the result that houseowners—sellers of shelter—were heavily penalised throughout the war, and incidentally encouraged to seek escape by various devices from the burden thus imposed upon them. The ' controlled price ' in this case was fixed by law rather than departmental action; in other cases prices were fixed by government departments, which clearly recognised that a controlled price was not necessarily an unvarying price.

The general level of controlled prices was determined by financial considerations. If the Government had not adopted the fatally easy plan of expanding the currency the shortage of supplies would alone have caused a rise in prices. There was less to go round, and competitors would have spent approximately the same amount of money in purchasing the smaller quantity of goods. But the Government repeatedly created fresh currency, which found its way as wages, salaries and profits into the pockets of the public, and the additional currency intensified the momentary demands of many fortunate individuals—ultimately the majority of the community. As the mere expansion of currency added to the supply of nothing else,

inevitable, under competitive conditions, during the process of currency expansion, results in a considerable demand for commodities, such as motor-cars or bicycles, the production of which is subject to increasing returns, and that their relative prices will therefore show a marked fall. The obverse is true of commodities subject to diminishing returns. But such cases do not often occur as the direct result of currency expansion.

prices mounted rapidly, and created the temptation to further expansion. This process had gone on for a considerable period before the prices of the bulk of foodstuffs were regulated, and the controlled prices were therefore fixed at a level appropriate to the volume of currency in circulation. No control was exercised over articles of clothing and certain other commodities, the prices of which were left to the higgling of the market, and tended to find their own level in the given circumstances. If no further expansion of currency had taken place, these might have become fairly stable, provided the supplies, though scanty, had remained fairly regular. But not only did the supplies tend to fall as the requirements for war increased, but the currency was further expanded and wages advanced. The new currency, finding no outlet on the market for controlled articles, added to the intensity of competition for uncontrolled articles, the prices of which therefore advanced not only absolutely, but relatively to those of foodstuffs, thus destroying the relationship which existed between prices in time of peace.[1] Thus it may confidently be stated that the abnormally high relative prices ruling to-day for such uncontrolled articles as clothing and furniture are largely due to the control policy in respect of foodstuffs. This statement is not meant to imply criticism either of the policy of controlling prices as far as possible or of the policy of expanding the currency within certain limits.

The Government was faced with serious difficulties, which were increased by its failure to impress upon the public the elementary fact that it was not possible,

[1] This relationship had already been seriously disturbed by differences in degrees of shortage and by the different degrees of persistence of demand through different ranges of prices.

while engaged in a conflict which demanded the undivided energy of the nation, to maintain that standard of living for the mass of the people which they had enjoyed in time of peace. The first difficulty was that of stabilising wages. The initial rise in prices, particularly in those of foodstuffs, combined with the increase in profits enjoyed by firms in industries essential for war, and in trades where the shortage was proportionately much less than the advance in prices, led to an irresistible demand for advances in wages. But such advances, although they led to a redistribution of purchasing power favourable to those who received them, and unfavourable to those in receipt of fixed incomes, did not reduce the shortage. They merely increased the competitive strength of workers for the scanty supplies, intensified the rise in prices and further increased the profits of producing and selling firms. The further rise in prices led to a second demand for advances, which was conceded, and produced the same result. And so the dog went on chasing its own tail. To change the metaphor, labour sought that will o' the wisp, the pre-war standard of living, and was assisted by the Government. Both were drawn into the morass. It was thought, when the Food Control Department had effectively controlled prices and rationed foodstuffs, that the Government and labour had not only escaped from the morass but also captured the glow-worm. Other necessaries, however, were left to the higgling of the market, and their prices continued to rise, and with them the 'cost of living.' And it is significant that general wages rates advanced more rapidly during the control period than they had done before. Moreover, by raising the cost of production they necessitated the periodic revision of the controlled prices of goods produced in this country. Wages were the main channel through which the new currency travelled ; but most of it reached the retailers, and percolated through to the wholesale dealers and producers. It is, of course, true that Government contractors were well paid—often exceptionally well paid—for their work ; but as the costing system improved and more and more establishments were brought under direct control, and their contracts more expertly supervised, their power of exploiting the needs of the nation was restricted, so much so that in the chief industries—such as engineering and iron and steel production—the State was compelled to accept contingent financial responsibility for the additional cost incurred through national advances in wages rates. Moreover, the munitions levy (which was ultimately merged in the excess profits duty) restricted the excess profits retainable by those firms controlled by the Ministry of Munitions to one-fifth of the pre-war standard. It is therefore extremely probable that, in spite of the excess profits duty, the bulk of the excess profits made during the war, and retained by the firms, were made in industry and commerce not directly connected with the supply of munitions of war. And the magnitude of such excess profits suggests that the majority of wage-earners acted mainly as post offices for the new currency periodically issued by the Government in response to the demands of the trade unions.

The question naturally arises whether the policy of giving periodic advances and so inflating the currency was a wise one ; and the reply involves the consideration of the second and third difficulties which faced the Government in its attempt to regulate the currency and the prices of necessaries. The second difficulty arose from the fact that price control without the control of supplies was bound to fail. Many necessaries of life, such as wheat, sugar, tea, coffee, etc., are obtained wholly or largely from abroad. Simple price control of an imported commodity might drive the commodities from our market. If the controlled prices were fixed below those obtainable abroad, imports would cease : for it should not be forgotten that there was a world shortage, if not of each individual commodity, at least of shipping for its transportation. The two alternatives before the Government were first to fix a price sufficiently high to outbid foreign competitors for the same article, leaving shipping free to accept the most profitable trade, which would then be trade with ourselves ; and, secondly, to purchase in bulk from foreign producers at the world price, 'ration' shipping to the extent required, and sell to the public at home at a fixed price below the purchase price, charging the deficit to the national account. The second alternative, involving what is known as a subsidy, was chosen. The subsidy is not a new invention. Its merits were discussed by Adam Smith nearly a century and a half ago. But the subsidy of the past was always a bounty either to exporters competing in a foreign market, and thus intended to foster the export trade, or, as is sometimes proposed for agriculture, to assist home producers in their competition against imports. But the new subsidies, such as that on wheat, are of a wholly different character, being in effect a bounty paid to foreign producers to induce them to send goods to this country. It is only conceivable in respect of necessaries of life during a period when their supply is dangerously small. But there is a limit even to the amount of subsidy which a nation can afford. If bread had continued to be sold at the pre-war price, the subsidy upon wheat purchased from abroad would have been vastly greater. For the world price would still have been determined largely by the currencies of other countries. And this indicates the third difficulty which faced the Government—namely, that no single state, trading with other states, is entirely a free agent in the control of its currency.

It is an axiom in economics that there is a strong tendency towards a common level of prices in countries trading with each other, due allowance being made for differences in their tariff policies and in the cost of transport. As this consideration has a strong bearing upon the present adverse position of our rate of exchange with America, and the difficulty of recovering our foreign trade, it requires very careful examination, although in these pages nothing more than a brief summary is possible. If we assume that all nations trading with each other employ gold, and only gold, as currency, it is clear that a continuous adverse 'balance' of trade would be followed by an export of gold in payment of the excess of imports. The loss of some gold would enhance the value of the remainder, that is, cause a fall in prices. Such fall would make this country a less profitable market for foreign producers and our imports would thus diminish. Moreover, in consequence of the fall in prices relatively to those prevailing abroad our exporting manufacturers would be in a stronger competitive position and our exports would increase, until ultimately their total value would exceed that of our imports, and the gold would return to this country. The statement is not rendered less true by the fact that gold is supplemented by credit currency. The latter is limited by gold,[1] and any serious withdrawal of the precious metal is followed by

[1] See Chapter III.

a contraction of credit currency, which, moreover, is only useful in foreign trade so long as it is convertible into gold.

Just as internal credit currency economises the use of gold and facilitates trading between firms, so, too, international credit currency economises gold as international currency and facilitates trading between nations. The chief form of such currency is the foreign bill of exchange, which is essentially a promissory note and will be so regarded for the purpose of simplicity. Suppose, for example, a British steel firm sends rails to the New York Corporation and receives a promise to pay three months hence, and a wheat importer imports wheat from Chicago of the same value. Both creditors expect to be paid ultimately in gold, or at least in the convenient currencies of their own countries. The shipment of gold to or from America is both risky and costly, and is clearly avoided if the wheat importer buys the promissory note from the steel firm and sends it by registered post to his Chicago creditor who in turn collects the money from the New York Corporation. Rather than incur the risk and cost of shipping gold it would be better for the wheat importer to purchase the promissory note at a slight premium. And if the steel firm is to be ultimately paid in New York and has to bear the cost of transporting the gold to this country it would pay him to sell the note at a small reduction. Each of the four parties represents a large group of traders of various kinds. If our imports from America exceed our exports, there are more people wanting such promissory notes than there are notes, which will be sold at a premium. The steel firm would thus make greater profit than 'expected,' some of it being the premium, that is, profit on exchange; and in the ordinary course exports would be stimulated. The wheat importer would be paying more for wheat by the amount of the premium, and imports would be discouraged, and the balance of trade would thus tend to be restored. It will thus be seen that when the 'balance of trade,' or the rate of exchange, is unfavourable we tend to pay higher prices in our home market for imported goods.

A Bank of England or Treasury note, when it finds its way to a foreign country, is regarded merely as a promissory note—a 'sight bill'; and its value fluctuates with the rate of exchange. If America has been exporting more to us than she has been importing from us, there will be more 'promissory notes' on sale than can find a market, and their price will fall. That is the position to-day, and it accounts for the fact that 'British money' has depreciated in America. It is not the gold sovereign—which of course is always and everywhere worth the gold it contains—but British Government and commercial paper, that has depreciated. During the war we imported essentials to the amount required, or possible, at fabulous prices, without being able to export goods in payment. Part payment was made by the sale of foreign securities—mainly American—held in this country, and by the creation of special loans in the United States, the proceeds of which were employed in payment of accounts. But there remains a considerable debit balance, which is the cause of the unfavourable rate of exchange—the measure of the depreciation of British credit money in America. The fall in value of credit documents of one country in another country may not, however, be wholly due to an adverse balance of trade. It may be accentuated by the feeling of uncertainty as to the debtor's ultimate solvency—that is, his ultimate power of restoring the balance of trade or paying the difference in gold. It is probable that this consideration does not at present influence the rate of exchange between this country and America ; but it might do so if industrial disturbances became more frequent or showed signs of becoming a permanent feature of British society ; as for the time being it has affected the credit of Russia in other countries. Risk of insolvency and repudiation on the part of the debtor state became a factor entering into the rate of exchanges, and was a factor during the war in the price of German Government credit documents, the value of which fell in the international market with every serious defeat.

It may be replied that the above considerations are purely financial, and do not seriously affect the average citizen. On the contrary, they are of profound social significance. If we are continuously to enjoy the benefit of American economic resources the balance of trade must finally be restored. This can be done in three ways: by the export of gold, the sale of remaining securities, or the export of goods. The first cannot continue indefinitely, and already we have depleted our gold reserves in this manner, almost to the limit of safety. Moreover, we have already disposed of a large proportion of our holdings abroad, and therefore lost a considerable sum per annum in interest payments, and incurred an annual obligation in interest payments in respect of the war loans floated in the United States. It is therefore necessary to export goods, if not to America at any rate to other countries which will provide means of discharging our debt to America. And, if we are to obtain our pre-war imports of food, raw materials, and other commodities upon which our standard of living depends, and to continue to export capital to other countries, our total exports must be sufficient to make up for the net loss of interest from abroad, and the loss on shipping and financial services which we have probably suffered during the war. The essence of the matter is that we called the tune in America, and must now pay the piper. By drawing upon America for essentials we put off to that extent the burden of war : we must now shoulder that burden.

The restoration of the export trade is bound up with the question of inflation. Our currency has been considerably expanded during the war, and such expansion is reflected in high wages, high costs, high prices and large profits. High prices reduce our competitive strength as a nation relatively to that possessed by a nation in which no such expansion of currency has taken place. It is stated that our engineering and steel firms cannot compete with their American rivals in neutral markets where, before the war, we held a commanding position. If such is the case it must be due to one or a combination of two causes. The first is such improvement in American methods of production that the economy of human energy employed in the manufacture of an article is greater than that effected by the competing industry in this country. The second cause is a currency which has not been expanded during the war to the same degree as ours, with the result that the rise in wages and costs has been less pronounced. In so far as this competitive impotence is due to the first cause it calls for greater inventiveness from our manufacturers and greater output per unit of energy expended—a result which is conditioned by the active co-operation of all workers. Even where it is due to the second it confers an initial advantage upon America ; but not necessarily a permanent advantage except in so far as success breeds success. Provided foreign purchasers possess adequate means of payment America will enjoy a boom in export trade, and her exporting firms will reap abnormal profits. But first the workers concerned will claim a share of such profits in the form of advances in wages, and secondly the prices of goods remaining in the country will advance with the shortage consequent upon the sudden pull by foreign markets, and the general body of workers will demand that the increase in the cost of living be followed, if not anticipated, by advances in wages. The currency will therefore expand.[1] The United States, during this process of expansion, will probably experience the same economic reactions as we did in 1916 and 1917, but they may be more rapid. Already coming events are casting their shadows before and the Government at Washington is striving to profit by our experience.

Thus we are brought back to the third difficulty which faced our Government during the war. If, in spite of the degree to which other states were inflating their currency we had attempted to restrict ours almost within pre-war limits ; if we had set our faces against advances in wages ; controlled prices at a much earlier stage ; fixed controlled prices at lower levels, and, in order to do this, subsidised our foreign purchases far more heavily, our position would have been like that of America. At the termination of the war, when nations resumed trade intercourse on a purely commercial basis, our currency would have

[1] This general result would be avoided if, first, private owners of capital in America granted loans to foreign countries to enable them to meet their obligations to American exporters ; or, secondly, the American government granted the loans and obtained the necessary amounts from the real savings of its own people.

rapidly expanded ; prices would have soared upwards ; the rapid and considerable advances in wages necessitated by such price movement would have been the subject of serious disputes, and controversies would have been embittered by the making of enormous excess profits during the process. Moreover, the subsidies might conceivably have added to the net burden of the national debt, in spite of the fact that purchases on government account from home manufacturers have been made at far lower prices.

Experience alone will show whether the policy of currency expansion was pursued too far, or far enough. If our currency has not been expanded approximately to the extent characteristic of our best customers, it may be further expanded before it is finally contracted. The contraction, when it begins, will assume an international character. No single nation is entirely a free agent in this matter, which is eminently suitable for control by the League of Nations. Our currency policy will be determined largely by that of other countries, an economic truth the force of which America is now beginning to realise, and which all industrial communities might have realised in the years immediately preceding the war. But the nation whose currency has been expanded less than the average is in a fortunate position. It stands a greater chance of recovering its export trade rapidly, and is less likely to experience the full force of a financial collapse. Provided the volume of currency is fairly constant, or varies but slowly, and the gold foundation is sufficiently strong, the actual volume is not a matter of the first importance, except to those in receipt of incomes which have not increased proportionately to the currency. Most people, indeed, prefer large incomes and proportionately high prices to small incomes and proportionately low prices.[1] The chief danger is that the gold foundation will not be sufficiently large and strong to bear the credit currency erected upon it, and that when the convertibility of paper money is generally restored the latter will be shown to be worth less than its face value in gold. If such proves to be the case we may experience a world panic, and witness a general collapse in prices and wages.

2. LABOUR

It was to be expected that a long war which imposed the severest strain upon the economic resources of the country would have created labour difficulties, but the precise nature of those difficulties was foreseen by no one. The developments of the last ten years seem to suggest that the problems which the war revealed in their nakedness were at least as important as those which it created. The labour movement was accelerated rather than largely diverted from its line of direction; and we are now confronted with a situation which, apart from the shortage of goods and the problems of resettlement and dilution, would have presented itself in its main essentials even if peace had remained undisturbed. 'Direct action' and 'the control of industry' were questions which were already coming to the front before the outbreak of war. The rise in prices, combined with the inelastic wage agreements, had created an atmosphere favourable to 'revolutionary' thought and action; unofficial strikes and sympathetic strikes had already made their appearance, and the 'triple alliance' already been mooted. The 'class war' was being widely preached and the

[1] The burden of the national debt at different price levels is ignored.

authority of the governments of many trade unions was showing signs of weakening.

The labour problem during the war was similar in some of its essentials to the commodity problem. The supply of labour was inadequate, and became more so as the war proceeded. The shortage first became acute in the engineering and shipbuilding trades, where it was intensified by the restrictive customs of the craft unions and the workers in many individual establishments. It was the subject of negotiation between the unions and employers' associations, and afterwards of inquiry by the Committee on Production, which quickly discovered that the craft unions held the key to the solution of the difficulty. These negotiations and inquiry led to the famous 'Treasury agreement' of March 1915, whereby the unions consented to dilution of labour and surrendered, for the time being, the strike weapon. The miners were not at that time affected by the dilution agreement, and they refused to surrender their right to strike. The craft unions consented in face of the national emergency, recognising that the safety of the state represented a claim superior to that represented by the right to strike. It is probable that the miners' representatives felt that in surrendering their right to strike in deference to the national emergency they would appear to be surrendering it for all time. Coal-mining is an essential industry in which a prolonged cessation of work in time of peace might produce a national crisis, if not of the character at least of the intensity of the existing crisis, which was regarded as constituting sufficient justification for the surrender.

The terms of the Treasury agreement were embodied in the Munitions of War Act, which contained four provisions directly affecting industrial workers employed by firms to which the Act was applied. It provided for dilution of labour; it declared strikes illegal; it aimed at controlling the movement of labour by the institution of the 'leaving certificate,' and, finally, it prevented exploitation on the part of the workers by controlling wages. The last three provisions are essentially those which were applied in the case of foodstuffs and other necesaries, namely, preventing sellers from withholding supplies; rationing such supplies and controlling their prices. And dilution corresponded to the Government's effort to increase food supplies by stimulating production at home, purchasing abroad, and, in the case of wheat, ekeing out supplies by admixture with offal. There was method in what has been called the Government's madness. What appeared to be similar circumstances called for similar treatment. But there was one essential difference between the two cases; in the one the Government was dealing with inanimate objects, in the other with human beings; masses of human beings; organised and suspicious masses.

Dilution necessitated the formation of dilution committees among craftsmen, and these in some cases became nuclei of organisations for furthering the cause of industrial unionism. They were intended to assist in the regulation of the terms of employment of women and other dilutees. The general terms were implied in the Treasury agreement, which provided that dilution would not be accompanied by any 'cutting' of piece-rates, the issue within sight then being the position of dilutee piece-workers employed on shells and fuses. But the principle of dilution was soon more widely extended, and the Government, in the statutory Rules and Orders issued by the Ministry of Munitions, accepted, fully and frankly, the principle of 'equal pay for equal work.'[1] The translation of this principle into specific though general regulations, and the application of such regulations to individual establishments created many difficulties, which were not reduced by the failure on the part of some employers to apply the regulations in the right spirit, and the failure on the part of some workers and their representatives to realise that equal pay for equal work meant unequal pay for unequal work.[2] The problems raised by the employment of women on men's work were exceedingly complex and difficult, but, in spite of the unpopularity from which it suffered, it is probable that the government department which was responsible for their solution was as successful as any created during the war to deal with emergencies.

There was ample justification for the provision which imposed restraint upon the mobility of workers employed on munitions work. If the latter had continued to enjoy complete freedom of movement a proportion—probably a large proportion—would have charged what the market would bear (a phrase now shortly termed 'profiteering') and attached themselves to those employers willing to pay the highest wages. These might or might not have been the employers engaged upon the most urgent work; but even if they had been, they would have become overstocked with skilled workers while the establishments of other employers, also engaged on urgent work but not so fortunate in respect of their terms of contract, would have been depleted. But the system of leaving certificates roused strong antagonism among a large proportion of workers for one or more of four reasons. Some objected not to the principle

[1] But women were not granted the same war bonuses as men.
[2] See Chapter VIII.

of restriction but to the fact that the restriction was imposed by individual employers enjoying, in many cases, excess profits. Others objected to the sectional application of the principle and the freedom which employers and others appeared to retain. Admitted that a measure of industrial conscription was necessary, it should have been applied, it was argued, to both parties. Nor were they impressed by the fact that indirectly the employers were conscribed in no less measure. They felt that the leaving certificate was the real badge of conscription, and conscription of the worst form. Thirdly, keen resentment was aroused by the arbitrariness of some employers in the use of their powers.

Finally, a large proportion of skilled workers were employed during the war on time-work. Trained engineers had been promoted from the machines to the tool-room or to 'setting up' the machines which they themselves once operated but which were now operated by untrained men and women employed on piece-work. By the Treasury agreement the latter were guaranteed piece-rates previously paid to skilled workers on similar jobs; and being employed on repetition work and unhampered by shop customs limiting output, their production and weekly wages exceeded expectations, and frequently exceeded the weekly earnings of the skilled workers whose places they had taken and who themselves were employed mainly or wholly on work calling for more continuous employment of skill than in the days of peace. In the financial sense the promotion of these skilled workers thus frequently proved to be an Irishman's rise.

It should not be forgotten that the discrepancy between the earnings of skilled day workers and semi-skilled piece-workers was mainly the consequence of the Treasury agreement and the Government's faithful observance of its terms. But it created a deep feeling of discontent with the relatively low wages of the skilled group, and of resentment against the authorities for having instituted the policy of restriction, which prevented them from seeking more remunerative work on machines. The 'lightning' district committees of 1917 on Industrial Unrest were impressed by the importance of this factor and expressed the view that the system of leaving certificates should be abolished, and the discrepancy between the wages of skilled day and semi-skilled piece-workers removed. The Government acted upon their recommendations. Freedom of movement was restored and a committee was appointed to consider ways and means of removing the wages discrepancy, its activities being followed by the issue of an Order prescribing a bonus of 12½ per cent. on earnings to skilled engineers and moulders employed on time work.

The history of the few months following the issue of this Order, if it is ever written, will provide food for deep reflection. It is sufficient at this stage to point out that the bonus appeared to be the inevitable consequence of the abolition of the leaving certificate. Nevertheless it had a demoralising effect, and intensified rather than mitigated the severity of the labour crisis. It was followed by the very result which had been anticipated by some people. The corollary to the abolition of the right to strike and the restriction of freedom was the regulation of wages and the implied guarantee that the 'controlled' workers should not suffer through loss of 'bargaining power.' Moreover, restriction itself was necessary partly to prevent undue exploitation of their market by the workers, among whom the desire to 'profiteer' was neither greater nor less than among other groups in the community. And restriction of movement was an essential preliminary to the control of wages. When the leaving certificate was abolished there was serious danger that many skilled day-workers would seek more remunerative employment, particularly on semi-skilled piece-work, and that employers would compete for them; and it was probably anticipated that the prospect of a bonus would have a narcotic effect. It appears that it did stabilise conditions for the time being, but the granting of the bonus was immediately followed by irresistible demands for its extension to all day-workers, who believed that the moulders had been included as the result of a serious strike in that trade on the Clyde, and that their own title was as strong as that of the moulders. When the demand was conceded a compensatory bonus of 7½ per cent. for piece-workers was wrung from the Government. The application of the general terms of this order and supplementary orders to individual establishments created a vast amount of friction, and the value of systems of piece-work and collective bonus on output was largely reduced.

Nor was that all. The abolition of restraint upon movement enormously increased the difficulty of regulating rates of pay. It was not always necessary for a workman to leave in order to obtain a higher rate; the mere threat to leave or expectation on the part of a firm that such threat would be forthcoming was enough, if the contracts were sufficiently remunerative to bear an advance. The Government thus threatened to lose grip of the wages situation, and the re-establishment of control of movement became inevitable. Some firms paid relatively high wages, thereby attracting applicants for skilled work and exercising a disturbing effect upon the labour situation in their own districts. The Government therefore employed the method of 'embargo,' that is, prohibited such firms from employing any additional skilled workers on work which could be performed by dilutees. The workers naturally interpreted this action as an overt attempt to apply the principle of restriction in a new and secret (and therefore more obnoxious) form. The restriction imposed upon movement by means of the leaving certificate was open and 'above-board'; nor was it undemocratic. Restriction was inevitable and was accepted as such by the vast majority of thoughtful workmen, though it was a useful drum to beat when the insurgents of the labour movement wished to collect, and incite to strike, a mass of workers irritated by the way in which the system had sometimes been applied in practice, or by other factors regarded as grievances. But restrictions imposed in the hope that the workman will remain unconscious of their real purpose are undemocratic, and, when discovered, are regarded as intolerable by all alike.

The attempt to abolish strikes during the war failed. Soon after the Munitions of War Act was passed a serious conflict occurred in the South Wales Coalfield, which, in order to avoid a strike, was 'proclaimed' under the Act. Nevertheless, the strike occurred, and it was shown that while isolated individuals could be prosecuted, it was impossible, under the prevailing circumstances, to coerce a body of two hundred thousand workmen. The failure on the part of the Government to exert its authority exhibited the inherent weakness of its position, and showed that other groups, provided they were sufficiently large, might strike with impunity. There were many strikes among bodies of men employed on munitions works, but they were all unofficial strikes. An explanation of these strikes necessitates a brief reference to the shop-steward movement, one of the most obscure phases of recent labour history.

It would be presumption to attempt to disentangle all the essential facts of the situation and the ideas which lay behind the insurrectionary movement. It is doubtful, indeed, whether any one within the movement itself—or outside—is competent at the present stage to review it as a whole. Its progress was too rapid even for its leaders to guide it as they wished, or fully to understand it.

Before the war shop stewards were official representatives of the craft unions, who performed detailed administrative work, but generally possessed no power to negotiate with the firm on behalf of the men employed in the establishment. When dilution was introduced, 'shop' questions assumed considerable importance, the number of such official stewards was increased, and many dilution and general works committees were formed. At the same time—and largely for the same reason—the barrier between crafts was weakened, and new bonds between them were created. There arose essentially the same kind of co-operation, within the individual establishment, between the stewards of the various crafts unions as already existed (through the district 'joint committees,' which negotiated with the Employers' Federation) between the craft unions themselves. Further, the abolition of the right to strike was regarded as having destroyed the bargaining power of the unions and their leaders, and reduced their value as instruments for removing grievances. And there were many real grievances.

The irritated masses therefore appointed unofficial shop stewards, who were elected not by the individual crafts represented in the establishment, but by the workpeople as a whole irrespective of craft. Among those selected were frequently the official shop stewards who, when they took part in the movement, acted unofficially.

Meanwhile the engineering trades had become 'essential' or 'public utility' trades in the sense that continuity of output was necessary to progress in the war. The consequences of a prolonged stoppage of work would have been disastrous, and the miners' strike of 1915 had revealed the futility of any coercive measure for suppressing strikes in an industry of such a character operating under war conditions. The shop stewards therefore formed district organisations for the purpose of enforcing better conditions than could be secured by ordinary negotiations. Complaints were repeatedly made against the Government, particularly in respect of delays (often unavoidable) which constantly occurred in the settlement of outstanding questions. It is important to observe that the support accorded to the shop-steward movement by the vast majority of the strikers rested upon the belief that strikes of this character provided the only effective method of securing the Government's earnest attention to their own grievances. Whether or not the belief was well founded is now a matter mainly of historical interest. The important point is that the strikes were directed largely against the Government, not the employers.

But the facts enumerated do not provide the complete explanation of the shop-steward movement and the series of unofficial strikes during the war. For the first and most important of this series took place in the Clyde district in February 1915, before the right to strike had been surrendered.[1] This strike occurred while wages negotiations were in progress between the official representatives of the unions and the employers' Federation, and was led by a group of shop stewards who formed themselves into the 'Withdrawal of Labour Committee,' an ad hoc body which was not allowed to dissolve, but became the more permanent organisation known as the Clyde Workers' Committee. It remains in existence to this day, and was instrumental in achieving the still more serious strike of this year—to which reference will presently be made. In 1915 the Committee was able to influence a large group of men (employed in a number of important establishments) who were irritated by the rise in prices of foodstuffs, and the large profits which their own strenuous work was said to bring their employers, and, more particularly, by the delays which had occurred before their claim of the union for an advance in wages received consideration, and the protracted nature of the subsequent negotiations.

To many of the shop stewards, however, the strike represented more than a sign of impatience with the delays inherent in the conduct of negotiations between large organisations. It marked the dawn of a new era. They sought to destroy craft unionism, and to establish an industrial union for the Clyde engineering and shipbuilding industry. Nor was the industrial union more to them than a necessary intermediate stage in the reorganisation of modern economic society. The competitive system was to be destroyed. If the war conferred a new im-

[1] A full account of this strike, and the issues it raised, is given in an article ("Labour and the War"), by the present writer in the *Political Quarterly* for May 1915.

portance upon the industry, and gave a new urgency to the work, and so increased their power, so much the better. The opportunity was one which should not be neglected.

There appears to be little doubt that the 'revolutionary' leaders exercised considerable influence throughout the war, and that the necessities of the war, which made the industry approximate, for the time being, to the coal industry in respect of the need for continuous output, influenced their policy, which, as we shall find, underwent a remarkable change after the Armistice was declared and the need for a continuous supply of munitions ceased. But their success was largely due to the apparent impotence to which the official bodies had been reduced by the abolition of the right to strike; by the irritation which was caused by the rise in prices and the disappointing results of advances in wages; by the manner in which some employers abused their power of restricting movement and the autocratic methods sometimes employed in introducing dilution. Their strike policy was, however, indirectly encouraged by the Government, which boldly prosecuted individuals for breaking the law while ready to fly into a panic at the threat of a serious strike by a large body. The Government was both culpable and unfortunate: perhaps its misfortune in having to cope with so difficult a situation was greater than its culpability for avoidable errors. For it undoubtedly suffered through the pre-war fall in trade union stock, which seriously reduced the value of agreements entered into by the leaders on behalf of the men in a number of crafts.

The main features of the labour situation as it existed at the time of the Armistice and developed during the winter and spring may be shown by two important examples, the Clyde strike, and the miners' threat to strike. During the war there was a pronounced shortage of labour, and wages were controlled by the Government. The immediate effect of the Armistice was largely to reduce the demand for munitions, and thereby to create unemployment on a large scale, pending the adaptation of factories to the requirements of peace. The prospect of unemployment was like a nightmare to the workers, who feared the effect which it might produce upon wages in general, particularly when the ranks of the unemployed were swelled by the demobilisation of the army and navy. The future was as uncertain as it had been in the autumn of 1914. It called for emergency legislation, and two important temporary measures were passed. The first provided for the payment of unemployment benefit to those thrown out of work; the second—the Wages (Temporary Regulation) Act—stabilised wages and preserved (under another title) the arbitration tribunal which, during the war, had been responsible for determining the periodic advances granted to meet increases in the cost of living.

There seems to be little doubt that they had an important and beneficial effect at the time, for the echoes of the 12½ per cent. bonus and the embargo had not yet died away, and at the same time there was a strong feeling of resentment at the continued advance in prices. Moreover, the partial strike on the railways in September revealed the continued strength of the 'rank and file' movement. The emergency measures were regarded as preparing the way for a general scheme of reconstruction. In view of the heavy and unremitting toil which the war had entailed for the vast majority of civilians it was natural that the first question raised should be the length of the working week. The problem of reducing hours had already engaged the attention of both parties in many industries, and an agreement embodying the principle of the forty-seven hours week was concluded without much delay in the engineering and shipbuilding trades, and was followed by similar agreements in other trades. To conclude a general agreement is one thing; to apply it to varying conditions is another. The September railway strike and the friction which preceded it had already revealed the danger of ambiguously worded agreements. The workers affected by the engineering agreement regarding the reduction of hours believed, rightly or wrongly, that not only the weekly time wages but also the general conditions of work would remain unaltered—apart, of course, from the starting and finishing times. But some employers evidently believed otherwise, and introduced stricter time-keeping conditions, by disallowing the usual short period of grace, refusing permission to late-comers to work at all during the period for which they were late, and, in some cases, compelling the men to register attendance at their own shops or departments instead of at the factory gates. Small margins of this character are valued by factory workers just as much as by scholars and university students, and as much as the hurried morning visit to the coffee shop is valued by the city clerk; and their abolition created a strong feeling of resentment. Moreover, the early and hurried breakfast, and the long hungry wait till dinner predisposed many workers against the one-break system, which, in the case of families where there are children attending school, complicates domestic arrangements. Finally, the adjustment of wages consequent upon the reduction of hours gave rise to controversy. The time-rate per hour was raised proportionately to the reduction of hours (thus providing the same weekly wages as had been paid for the longer working week), and was thus fixed without difficulty. But as it was clearly understood that the output per week would not suffer it was argued that piece-prices and other rates of payment when such payment was by result did not call for readjustment. The workers affected thought otherwise. Moreover, in cases where a contractor paid an assistant (*e.g.* plater's helper) time-rates from the proceeds of his contract, the former held that as his contract or piece-price was not affected he could not be expected to pay the enhanced hourly rate to the latter, thus suffering a reduction of net payment to himself. Questions such as these were subjects of controversy and created a considerable amount of friction.

Finally, the amount of reduction in the hours of work per week (from 53 and 54 to 47) was less than that demanded in many places. During the war the Clyde District Committee of the A.S.E. had reported in favour of a post-war working week of 40 hours and a similar policy was adopted by the Scottish Trade Union Congress, while the (unofficial) Clyde Workers' Committee started an agitation for a 30-hours week. The events following the adoption of the 47-hours agreement and leading up to the strike of January are somewhat obscure ; but it is clear that there were various conferences between trade union committees of trades outside engineering, unofficial bodies, such as the Shop Stewards' Committee, and official bodies, such as the Glasgow Trades and Labour Council and the Scottish Trade Union Congress, which went beyond their ordinary functions in the matter.

There are several features of general and permanent importance connected with the strike which call for comment. The first is that the strike was partly official and partly unofficial. Some of the trade unions outside engineering 'recognised' and co-operated with the unofficial Clyde Workers' Committee and thus, in effect, declared war upon the A.S.E. The second is that the strike movement was inspired and fostered by the revolutionary body, which had declared in favour of a 30-hours week. The third is that the official district committee of the A.S.E. acted rebelliously against the parent society in throwing in its lot with the unofficial movement. This feature is of considerable importance in that it revealed the influence of the 'rank and file' movement and the weakening of authority on the part of the national executive even over its own district officials. Yet it is a testimony to the latent strength of the A.S.E. as a national craft organisation that in spite of the opposition of the extremists, the rebellion of its own district committee, and the alliance of other trade unions with the insurgent bodies, it not only survived the ordeal but emerged from it strengthened and able to exercise greater control than had been possible for some years before.

The fourth feature of the strike was that to many of the leaders it was mainly political. Those who regarded it in that light consisted of two groups, namely, the out-and-out extremists, whose aim was a strike and who found in the claim for a further reduction of hours a useful instrument for achieving their aim; and those whose disappointment with the political situation was so bitter as to cause them to preach and practice the gospel of 'direct action.' Any aggressive action which the latter group cared to propose would naturally be supported by the former, who aimed at making the present economic system unworkable by creating friction and fomenting strife whenever and wherever possible.

The fifth important feature was the introduction of ' mass picketing ' which enormously increased the difficulty experienced by non-strikers in entering and leaving the factory. ' Withdrawal of labour ' has long been a euphemistic description of a strike, the essence of which is not refusal to work but an endeavour, within the limits permitted by law, to prevent the industry from being carried on, or the factory from being kept at work. With ' mass picketing ' it becomes a perversion of the truth to state that a strike is mere withdrawal of labour. The method of ' persuading ' others to join is not that of appeal to reason but of terrorism.

Finally, the strike represented a serious attempt to create a local general strike. Sympathetic strikes were of frequent occurrence before the war : but they generally represented a spontaneous effort (or ready response) on the part of a body of men who had no special grievance against their own employers to assist those in another industry or occupation to secure conditions of work which they regarded as just. The situation on the Clyde was essentially different. Strong efforts were made by the strikers to ' persuade ' workers in other industries, essential to the community, *e.g.* the municipal tramways, to cease work. And it was no mere coincidence that action of this character was taken during a strike for shorter hours—a question affecting all workers, and most in like degree.

Reference has already been made to the fact that during the war the engineering industry became a ' public utility ' or ' essential ' industry in the sense that substantial continuity of output was necessary to the life of the community. The workers therein therefore possessed exceptionally strong bargaining power (as coal miners and railway workers do at all times), and the mere threat to strike was generally sufficient to call the serious attention of the Government to their claims. But before the war strikes and lock-outs, when they occurred, were generally of long duration, and ended in victory to the employers. The Clyde shop stewards realised that the Armistice had altered the essential features of the situation, and felt that if they reverted to the pre-war methods of bargaining—through the national executive—they might be faced with the same prospect of long struggles, under unfavourable conditions, with final defeat almost inevitable. They desired a short sharp struggle of a character which would force the Government to intervene, and to achieve this end by securing the co-operation of those employed in essential local industries such as lighting and tramways. A local general strike, which would make life intolerable, if not impossible, would prove more effective than a national engineering strike (if it could be achieved) as it would force the public to 'interfere' and possibly, too, compel surrender to the men's claims. Those leaders who emphasised this aspect of the strike were not, of course, the extremists who, following the Syndicalists of France, regarded the strike as the gateway to a new economic world. But they were more numerous, and probably more influential.

The Clyde strike may be regarded as an example of direct action, which means the employment of the industrial weapon for political purposes. But even more important was the threat of the Miners' Federation to strike to enforce their demands for nationalisation of the coal industry. In spite of its serious consequences, a strike for higher wages and a shorter working day would have resembled an ordinary industrial strike. But a strike to compel nationalisation would have been essentially a political strike. In essence the claim of the miners' leaders was that the attitude of the Government towards each industry should be determined, not by the will of the community but by the desire, at any moment, of the majority of the workers in that industry. If the steel workers wanted State ownership the State should nationalise the steel industry. If postal employees wanted the post-office denationalised it should be surrendered to private control. The community as a whole had no say in a matter of this kind: its own wishes were merely irrelevant.

It is clear that government under such conditions would be impossible. Even assuming the claim itself to be a strong claim, it seems clear that to compel its recognition by the Government through the method of coercion is the negation of democratic rule. Nor is it any reply to say that the case for nationalising the coal industry is overwhelmingly strong. The miners threatened to strike not because their claim was just but because they thought it to be just. Assuming State ownership and control to be extremely desirable in the view of all those best qualified to judge, the democratic method would be for the miners to convert expert opinion into national desire, not to coerce the community by the employment of force, whether it be physical or economic. A strike to secure this end does not differ, in principle, from the action of those seamen who (no less sincere than the miners) refused a passage to the Continent for those whose political views were not their own.

Nor is it a reply to say that the question of nationalisation is of the same nature as that of wages, and should therefore be dealt with in the same manner ; in other words, that the workers should be empowered to determine not only wages and hours of work, but also the form of ownership and control in their industry. Even critics of direct action are sometimes inclined to agree that this is a marginal or borderland case. But there is no intrinsic difference between ' industrial ' and ' political ' questions relating to industry. Advocates of the general strike recently defended their attitude by stating that all political questions are industrial—not only nationalisation, but even the ' Russian War.' The real truth is that all industrial questions are ultimately and in the wider sense political; that is, the manner in which industrial questions shall be dealt with is determined by the State, which means the community as a whole and not merely an industrial section of it. It is clearly the State which has to decide what is or is not a matter which can be left to private action, whether individual or collective ; and which it should retain—or recover—for settlement by itself. The right of ' self-determination ' in industry is derivative—a gift by the State ; and where, as in sweated trades before the war, and most trades during the war, the effects of its exercise were anti-social, the right was cancelled or restricted. The line of demarcation between ' political ' (narrowly interpreted) and ' industrial ' questions is thus drawn by the State itself. And the State—like every democratic body—has hitherto reserved to itself the task of determining the ultimate form of control for the industry, or the right of delegating that task to others.

It is therefore true to say that in threatening to strike for Nationalisation the Miners' Federation was adopting an attitude of hostility to democracy, and attempting to rule by force. It based its action not on the belief that the community as a whole desired State ownership (though that might serve as a pretext), but that the Federation itself wished it. And if, after experience of national control its view were to change, it would feel itself equally justified in threatening to strike for decontrol.

All this may be stated without denying the importance of the miners' attitude towards private ownership as one factor among many in determining the merits of nationalisation.[1] Moreover, it is possible that in demanding nationalisation the Miners' Federation was voicing the desire of the community. Both the community and the Government are faced with a serious difficulty, which is a legacy of the war. The difficulty is that the methods by which the political democracy once governed have become for the moment extremely unsatisfactory. The recent general election was fought on those issues which appeared to be the most important and urgent. But the new administration is being called upon to deal with a multitude of problems each of which involves a 'first-class' measure, and many of which contain implications of important philosophical principles which, under normal conditions, would be submitted to the electorate. It was assumed that emergency measures of reconstruction, like emergency war measures, could be devised which would not seriously prejudice the ultimate form of economic and social development. But the discovery has quickly been made that the abnormal problems cannot be completely divorced from or solved without reference to their inevitable consequent problems. The result is that the Govern-

[1] See Chapter VII.

ment finds it difficult to interpret the wishes of the community, and the community finds it impossible to articulate its 'general will.'

It was probably for this reason that a 'National Industrial Conference' was called by the Government for the purpose of examining the most urgent labour problems. If a representative gathering of employers and workpeople could arrive at an agreement upon the most urgent measures of industrial reconstruction there would be afforded strong presumptive evidence that such measures would receive the approval of the community. If the conference proved a success the way would be paved for the establishment of a permanent National Industrial Council. The proposed Council has been called an Industrial Parliament, but it could be no more than an advisory committee. Legislative functions could not be delegated to a body upon which no financial responsibility rested. As the Industrial Conference was able to submit agreed recommendations of the first importance, the experiment must be pronounced a success, and the method in keeping with democratic principle and procedure.

It was probably for the same reason that the Government so far surrendered to the threat of direct action by the miners as to appoint the Coal Industry Commission, upon which both employers and workpeople were represented. It was hardly to be expected that the Commission would issue a unanimous report upon the subject of nationalisation. The National Industrial Conference merely registered those measures upon which agreement had been reached ; it did not follow that such recommendations represented the full programme of either side. What some members would regard as the central issues were either not discussed, or, if they were discussed, were not the subject of joint recommendations. The Coal Industry Commission, on the other hand, was given specific terms of reference, being invited to investigate and report upon the central problem of control. It was not to be expected that the employers' representatives would report in favour of industrial suicide through nationalisation, or that the miners' representatives would surrender their position by reporting in favour of some alternative to nationalisation. The two sides represented policies as well as constituencies, and an impartial inquiry on their part was not to be looked for. On the other hand, the members included independent commissioners and there was an independent chairman. Moreover, the proceedings, unlike those of the Industrial Conference, were public. Two things might therefore be expected to follow. The first was that the publication of the evidence from day to day would create public opinion on the subject, so that before the report was published the 'general will' would be manifest. The second was that the recommendations of the independent commissioners would be interpretative of that general will. If these expectations had been realised the Commission would have proved an undoubted success. But they were not; and the reason is obvious. In the absence of full information upon the working of different forms of control in the same type of industries and *under similar conditions* (and such information is available for no industry in which the producing unit is not, as in the case of tramways, inherently monopolistic) judgment is apt either to be based entirely upon *a priori* reasoning, or to be largely influenced by supposed analogies which, upon examination, prove to be false or incomplete. The Commission received much evidence relating to the industry during the abnormal conditions created by the war; it received comparatively little evidence upon the experience of the industry under normal competitive conditions before the war—which would have been more strictly relevant to the issue.

CHAPTER VII

ECONOMIC REORGANISATION

1. Industry and the State

THE immediate economic task of the State (apart from the discharge of its economic responsibilities to other suffering States) is to secure an adequate supply of those goods and services upon which the welfare of the community depends. More is implied in that statement than the production of goods in large masses, for it is of the first importance that the right categories of goods be supplied. It was symptomatic of the early failure of the Government to grasp the nature of the problem of 'reconstruction' that some of the first groups of disabled soldiers were trained as diamond cutters and polishers. The shortage which it is important to relieve is that which exists in the necessaries and comforts of life; not until the supply of labour is adequate in those industries directly and indirectly concerned with the continuous provision of essentials will the nation be able to afford expenditure of labour energy upon the supply of extravagant luxuries. Some of the 'goods' essential to life and comfort are of a durable character, and quality is therefore of immediate concern. The need for a substantial increase in houses is as urgent as any. But the houses which will be erected during the next few years will determine the standard of comfort for a considerable proportion of the population for half a century. If, therefore, the State (which is responsible for the new housing policy) is in earnest in its endeavour to improve social conditions, it will secure that the new houses erected for the ' working classes ' will be better in every way than those in which the majority now live. They will be a lasting symbol of the standard of living which we believe the wage-earners of the next generation should enjoy.

The housing problem, in its financial aspect, presents great difficulty. The new houses will be erected during a period of expanded currency, and therefore at abnormally high costs. It may be assumed that such costs will not provide more than ' reasonable ' profits to the contractors and those who supply materials, and that their excess over pre-war costs therefore represents advances in wages and salaries, together with that increase in interest charges represented roughly by the rise in the net rate of interest on Government loans. On that assumption and the further assumption that the currency will remain equally expanded for many years to come (and that existing wages rates will thus be maintained) there appears to be no argument for subsidising housing schemes. The proposed Government subsidy is to be defended on the ground that one or both of these assumptions are likely to prove false. It thus appears that the Government anticipates a contraction of currency, and that it aims at 'writing off,' as a war loss, the difference between the cost of building in the immediate future and the cost after the currency (and price level) has been reduced to the new normal condition. If this anticipation proves to be true, the policy of the Government will have been justified. If, however, the general price level does not fall, the policy of subsidising housing construction will be in danger of becoming permanent.

But that is not all. The cost of building dwelling-houses before the war tended to advance more rapidly than the cost of producing manufactured articles. There was less scope for economising human energy by inventiveness and the introduction of machinery. Advances in wages and labour cost were followed by advances in total cost. House rents thus tended to become larger rather than smaller individual items in the household budgets. Industrial progress should find expression in a reduction in the relative importance of each individual item, thus making room for new items. Little or no progress was being made in the method of construction of dwellings. Hence the tendency to erect jerry-built houses. If, therefore, the Government is to improve upon the efforts of the past and at the same time to charge what will ultimately prove to be an 'economic rent,' it is clear that either real economy must be sought by the introduction of better methods of construction or the community must be prepared to accept house rent as a relatively more important item of the household budget. As the former is not likely to be achieved it is not unlikely that house rents in the future will show an advance upon pre-war rents greater than that shown in wages.

The housing problem illustrates the difficulty of separating the emergency measures of reconstruction from those by which they will be followed. During the war Government departments endeavoured to 'prejudice' as little as possible the consideration of post-war policy; but both on the labour and commercial sides they were swept along by the forces created or liberated by the war, which, by revolutionising economic conditions, has also compelled or hastened far-reaching changes in economic policy. Those which call for consideration include the shortage of goods and services, the organisation of industry, expansion of currency, the future of wages, and the recovery of international trade. Each of these is closely related to the others, and all are affected by the feeling of uncertainty which now prevails.

It is clear that so long as the shortage of foodstuffs remains acute in the world, or shipping for their transport seriously inadequate, State control of prices and distribution will inevitably continue.[1] Moreover, so long as States compete against each other for the surpluses of exporting nations, we shall be compelled either to continue existing subsidies on necessaries or allow prices to rise to the level determined by world prices. If the latter policy is adopted, farmers and other groups in this country will reap enormous profits. Moreover, the rise in the cost of living will lead to further advances in wages, which in turn may seriously retard the recovery of foreign trade. This constitutes one of the chief elements of uncertainty during the transition period.

In a world which is suffering from the destructive effects of war, and in which schemes of material development have been suspended for five years, there is obviously a greedy market for the products of all nations, provided such products are offered in the right proportions. But it is extremely unlikely that they will be offered in the right proportions. Some of the most important industries in time of peace acquired still greater importance to belligerent States during the war. For example, new factories were erected in the United States and this country for the manufacture of spelter, and it is likely that the pro-

[1] About the same time as the intention of raising the blockade against Germany was published, the Government announced its (then) policy of abolishing the control of foodstuffs !

ducing capacity of the world was enormously increased, and is now far in excess of requirements. The case of the manufacture of chemical products and dyes has been sufficiently canvassed. During the war, too, the production of iron and steel was considerably increased. We witnessed, in short, a one-sided development of industry which is likely to present a difficult problem during the next few years. Industries essential for war as well as peace have grown more rapidly than the world's requirements for their products. Keen international competition may therefore be expected, which has already been foreshadowed in the eagerness for new markets displayed by the American firms in the metal industries. Every advance in wages without corresponding increase in output constitutes a handicap to competing manufactures in this country. During the transition period, therefore, the policy of stabilising the cost of living by continuing subsidies would prove advantageous to those industries and constitute an indirect subsidy to the manufacturers. The alternative might be failure even to recover pre-war markets—much less discover new markets to absorb the additional production—followed either by serious unemployment or considerable reductions of relative wages. The problem is that of redistributing industrial effort to meet the requirements of peace. Farmers are lacking in confidence because they are unable to estimate the intensity of foreign competition when all trade restrictions are abolished and normal conditions in other countries are restored. But they are at least aware that their industry is not overgrown. Metal manufacturers, on the other hand, are exposed to the still more serious risk that the world requirements may fall short of the existing producing capacity of the world, and that for some years they may be faced with ruinous competition. Nor would import restrictions solve the difficulty; for the chief competitive market will be abroad. The problem, moreover, is not merely that of currency expansion and the relative levels of general prices in different countries. If the various currencies were reduced to their pre-war levels the difficulty would remain. For it has been created by the sudden expansion of a secure market which will again not only be seriously contracted but thrown open to all competitors. Vested interests have been created in the world of capital and that of labour, and the problem of commercial policy may need to be reconsidered in the light of this fact. It has already been pointed out that the new economic policy will be largely influenced by political considerations. If the League of Nations is not accepted as sufficient insurance against the risk of war it is probable that 'essential industries' will be fostered. If any special treatment which they may receive is granted for political reasons, it becomes part of the policy of defence and is of the nature of expenditure upon armament. Economic considerations become essentially subordinate.

If it be assumed that for political reasons it is desirable to foster such industries, their relation to the State will naturally call for special consideration; for there must be adequate guarantee that the protection is not abused, either by employers or workmen. Protection may be granted by restricting competing imports or by providing direct or indirect subsidies. The latter is the only possible alternative if the industry is to live partly by exporting its products. Most key industries are of a kind which may be carried on in this country without serious geographic disadvantages; their success depends more upon technical research, industrial education and courageous policy. In such cases the endowment by the State of specific education and industrial research would be a form of indirect subsidy which (on the assumption that political considerations necessitate some form of protection to key industries) would meet with general approval. Even a direct subsidy possesses advantages which are lacking in import restrictions, for it would enable the State to exercise more effective control upon development and to prevent protection from becoming the instrument of extorting abnormal profits or excessive wages from the community.

The extent to which the community has suffered from 'profiteering' during the last few years has given fresh impetus to the demand for nationalisation. Not only is it contended that no essential industry should be artificially protected, by subsidy or otherwise; it is further held that certain standardised industries (among which key industries are to be reckoned) should be taken over by the State, to be operated as public services. It is noticeable, however, that profiteering is due not to competition but to the suspension of competition, for which shortage was responsible. 'Profiteering' appears to mean charging what a strong market will bear when supplies are inadequate, that is, charging the highest possible price for which all available supplies can be sold.[1]

If the State does not control price and ration the commodity the only available alternatives to the seller are to charge a price which repels surplus demand or to

[1] The position of sellers has been strengthened by lack of knowledge on the part of buyers regarding the extent of the shortage, which in many cases is enormously magnified by the prevailing prices.

ration his own customers. The latter policy would be impossible in the case of furniture, clothing and other costly commodities purchased at infrequent intervals, and futile in the case of small ' repeat orders ' without guarantee that the customer would not augment his stock by purchase elsewhere. Even if the State had nationalised the wholesale and retail industries it would probably have been compelled to adopt the same general policy or undertake an elaborate and extremely perilous rationing policy which would entail an excessive expenditure of labour energy. High prices appeared to be the simplest method of enforcing economy, and the excess profits duty an effective instrument for preventing individual ' profiteers ' from retaining a disproportionate share of the accidental surplus. Effective competition, which implies the possibility of providing adequate supplies at a price equal to the cost of production, would have prevented the continued enjoyment of such excess profits. The value of the competitive system in time of peace is thus to be estimated not by the experience of the last five years but by its results under normal peace conditions.[1]

Nor does experience of State control during the war throw much light upon the problem of nationalisation. The partial control of the coal industry has been condemned by the chairman of the Coal Industry Commission. Probably it combined the evils of private

[1] The above paragraph is not a defence of ' profiteering.' It merely points out the dilemma of the seller—be it of goods or labour—who endeavours to carry out what he conceives to be his duty. Anti-profiteering shops sell at prices below those prevailing in the open market—and ' sell out' very quickly. Provided the shortage remains acute, the Anti-Profiteering Act will simply revive the queue system or its equivalent. It does nothing to remove the evil.

and State ownership without securing the advantages of either. More encouraging conclusions have been drawn from the experience of the Ministry of Munitions. But the task of organising for war was far more simple than would be that of serving the unknown ends of peace production. The 'market' of the Ministry was inexhaustible and therefore presented no risks. The products were highly standardised and of uniform quality. The organisers were, in the main, people who had been trained in competitive industry. Everybody was working under the stimulus of war, and the majority employed in munitions industries were prepared for sacrifices which could only be expected at such a time. The sole test of success was an adequate and continuous supply of munitions. The methods employed were frequently those which would invite failure in time of peace. On the other hand, the delays on the part of Government to secure the rapid construction of houses during the present abnormal year should not be regarded as illustrative of the inevitable result of State enterprise.

The strength of the argument for State ownership in an individualistic State depends largely upon the nature of the industry. Industries may be classified for practical purposes according to whether (*a*) they are essential (in the sense that substantial continuity of output is essential to the life and comfort of the community) or non-essential; (*b*) they are inherently monopolistic or competitive; (*c*) their products are standardised or varied. An 'essential industry' such as a tramway enterprise in a large city is inherently monopolistic in the sense that two systems serving the same area would involve extravagant waste. An uncontrolled private monopoly would therefore be a serious menace to the community, and, partly for this reason, the enterprise is generally regarded as intrinsically suitable for public control. The nature of the industry renders such control or management relatively simple. The railways of this country fall into the same category. They have long been regulated by the State, which now appears to have adopted the policy of stricter control almost amounting, in effect, to State management. The tailoring trade lies at the other extreme. It is not essential, in the special sense in which the term is here employed ; it is intrinsically competitive, and its products are extremely varied. Consequently it has not received any special attention from those who advocate nationalisation.

Intermediate between these extremes are the coal-mining and iron and steel manufacturing industries. Coal-mining under present conditions is an essential industry. The product is a gift of nature, and may thus be regarded as standardised. But the industry is inherently competitive. There is, indeed, no industry in which a private monopolistic trust would experience such great difficulties or in which an attempt to form such a trust would be so likely to fail. Under present conditions the industry is, moreover, highly speculative. Demand, which varies for reasons not connected with prices, is such that, where it appears, it is tenacious and persists through considerable changes in price. Supply, though affected by the opening or closing of mines, is similarly inelastic for short periods. A slight disturbance of either supply or demand tends to produce considerable variations in price, which thus fluctuates violently. The fluctuations are often intensified by market operations. The consequence is that the energies of firms are largely devoted to encountering commercial difficulties which would be largely reduced by concerted action. Fortunes are made and lost on the commercial side of the undertaking. The last few years before the outbreak of war were exceptionally profitable years in this industry, and provided a favourable standard for the assessment of war profits retainable by individual firms.

Coal-mining is a distinctly unpleasant occupation. The work itself is generally laborious, and carried on under unfavourable conditions. It will be generally agreed that, although his work may not involve skill comparable to that required of a toolmaker or coppersmith, the miner should, and, under strictly competitive labour conditions, would receive relatively high wages. Although reliable statistics of average pre-war earnings do not appear to be available, it is stated that they were relatively low. The statement is probably true of a proportion of miners ; if it is generally true the nation obtained its coal at an unduly low price. Moreover, the housing conditions in a large number of exclusively mining communities were, and continue to be, a disgrace to modern civilisation. The combination of circumstances briefly described has led to a strong demand for nationalisation. This demand, as distinguished from the demand for unification, has been supported by two arguments which are applicable to all important industries. The first is that the State would be able to substitute the best method of production in all units for those now existing. Under competitive conditions the prices determining costs are those which prevail in the badly equipped factories or mines. Only a small proportion of the latter are equipped with the most modern appliances. Competition has thus itself failed as a method of organising production. Opponents of nationalisation reply that it is of the essence of industrial progress that a small minority should lead.

What is a well-planned and well-equipped works to-day may be regarded as badly organised twenty years hence. But if the industry were nationalised and conditions stereotyped there might be no change in the meantime, and the modern plants of to-day might remain apparently the last word in industrial organisation. In other words, there is no prospect that nationalisation would provide an effective substitute for the enterprising firms which now 'set the pace.' What value should be attached to these views it is extremely difficult to determine by appeal to history. No industry which is intrinsically competitive has yet been controlled by the State. Further, the experience gained by the State or municipality in operating industries intrinsically monopolistic—such as the post office or a tramway system—is not necessarily a reliable guide to the prospects which other industries similarly conducted would enjoy. The problems presented by the former are comparatively simple. Moreover, State control of a few industries in an industrial society based upon economic freedom differs from State control of all industries as a substitute for economic freedom.

It is noticeable, however, that efficient organisation, whether by the State or by private enterprise, implies diversity rather than uniformity of methods of production. When a plant has once been erected it must be allowed to run for a time without serious interference. If the machinery were scrapped every time a new method was discovered the plant would always be in the hands of constructional engineers, never employed in manufacturing the goods which it was intended to produce. This neglected point seems to be of considerable importance, for it is probable that in many highly competitive industries which exhibit diversity of method in manufacturing similar products the differences signify the fact that in the circumstances under which they appear the less modern methods remain, for the time being, the most economical, from the standpoint of society as well as that of the individual firm. Nevertheless there is considerable evidence in support of the view that in some industries competition has not had the stimulating effect commonly attributed to it. This is due in part to secrecy, which has been regarded as of the essence of competition; and in part to the fact that the substitution of new for existing methods of production would involve an enormous increase in capital expenditure, perhaps necessitating the formation of a joint-stock company, and the choice of a new site in another part of the country, or in another country. Such appears to be the explanation of the many antiquated blast furnaces still in operation in this country.

The second argument employed in support of nationalisation is that it would produce a strong and lasting effect upon the workpeople. Working for the State they would be working for the community rather than apparently for the benefit of the private employer. The stimulus provided by the feeling that they were employed in public service would be reflected in their work. The strength of this argument is susceptible of adequate test. If municipal employees and State servants have a stronger sense of moral obligation and are more efficient than people employed in similar occupations by private firms, there is a strong presumption that the simple fact of being directly employed by the community is of profound psychological significance. But there is no evidence that such is the case. Moreover, the experience even of national projectile factories during the war suggests that the sense of public service did not provide so strong a stimulus as payment by results.

The argument, when applied to the coal-mining industry, is stated in a slightly different form, which gives it an entirely new significance. It is held that the vast majority of the miners resent the competitive organisation so deeply, and desire nationalisation so strongly, that there appears to be little hope for the future unless the industry is taken over by the State; in other words, they will only be efficient workers if they become State servants. If the statement is true, and likely to remain true, it constitutes a very strong argument for nationalisation.[1] The function of the State is not to preserve the competitive system, but to secure the most effective organisation of production, taking all factors into consideration. The first element in industrial efficiency is goodwill on the part of the workers. If in any industry the general and permanent result of competition is resentment and unwillingness to provide efficient service, the system in that industry must be pronounced bankrupt. The most modern appliances and the best technical education are of no avail if they are not reinforced by efficient work on the part of the wage-earners. It is difficult, however, to estimate the strength of this feeling among the miners, and, if it is strong to-day, to determine whether it is likely to remain strong, and as strongly in favour of nationalisation as it is in opposition to the present system. There are many alternatives to State ownership and control; the form of control now advocated

[1] I refer not to the employment of coercive measures, such as direct action, to secure nationalisation, but to the feeling of despair which the competitive system is said to have produced, and its subtle reaction upon the efficiency of the miners.

by the Miners' Federation is not the same as that proposed a few years ago. Experience of State ownership and control might itself in a few years create a feeling of antagonism no less strong than that now said to prevail against the competitive system.

The coal industry provides a suitable field for simultaneous experiments of different kinds, and acceptable to a body of workers desiring a change of system. There are several distinct coal-bearing areas, differing in geological features and probably in economic characteristics. These areas are sufficiently distinct to be regarded as economic entities for the purpose of experiment. One coalfield might be nationalised. Advocates of nationalisation would thus be provided an opportunity of testing their theories under the most favourable circumstances, and miners would gain valuable experience of State management in practice. Experiments of a different kind might be tried in other areas.

In evidence before the Coal Industry Commission I submitted the following scheme for trial in a selected coal-field. A Kartel or Joint Board should be formed, " upon which equal representation would be given to employers, workpeople, consumers and the State (which would also be the chief consumer). Its function would be to purchase the coal from the mine-owners and sell it to the consumers. The purchase price would be quoted 'free on truck,' and vary only according to quality.

" The difference between the purchase price and sale price (free on truck), would represent expenses of management plus a contribution towards a special compensation fund. The Board would distribute orders to the mine-owners, the individual quota being determined at first by the producing capacity of the mine; but the owner would be permitted to supply additional quantities at prices below the fixed or standard price, the excess to be permitted varying with the extent of the reduction in price—thus x tons at 1s. per ton reduction shillings $(x+y)$ tons at $(a+b)$ 1s. per ton reduction, and so on. Stocks would thus be accumulated. Under normal conditions the subsequent quota of the mine would be increased *pro rata*, and the standard price adjusted. This would prevent owners from 'dumping' during depression, for the subsequent regulated uniform or standard price would be affected thereby. Yet each firm would quote as much as possible below the standard price in order to retain its quota. The position of the individual mine-owner would be (to use a technical phrase) similar to that of a monopolistic combination producing manufactured goods, the demand for which is highly elastic—which is a consummation to be desired.

"The standard price would be determined at first substantially by the conditions prevailing in *relatively* poor mines—to be more precise (for it is a vital point) by the average cost of mining, say, that half of the total supply which is most costly to produce. (The fraction is purely illustrative.) But the quota of the richer mines would gradually increase, and the standard price gradually fall (see last paragraph).

"There would therefore be needed a subsidy for the poorer mines, drawn from the profits of the Board. The subsidy would be *pro rata* with output, not producing capacity, and there would probably be reached in some cases a point at which a reduction in price, plus fair compensation for closing down a mine, would be better than the maintenance of the standard price. This would be in line with the present custom of scrapping machinery in manufacturing industries ; it would avoid the danger of a reduction in wages rates; it would prevent the sudden closing down of mines, allow workmen time to adjust themselves to new conditions, and preserve mines in existence as long as socially desirable; it would provide compensation to the owners where necessary, and stimulate enterprise; it would considerably reduce the increment in profits due to geographic conditions, and prevent that due to trade booms; it would stabilise prices (free on truck), and eliminate the speculative element, while securing a gradual downward tendency in relative prices. Mine-owners, with a fairly assured market (yet one susceptible of relative growth) would concentrate upon industrial management, success in which would determine whether or not there would be growth. The Board would institute and maintain a Research and Commercial Institute, and the results would be available to all." It was further proposed that pithead committees should be extended and strengthened, and that in each firm "a workers' delegate should be appointed as member of the Board of Directors. There are objections to this policy, even when the commercial function has been so largely taken over by the area Board; but they do not appear to outweigh the argument in favour of experiment along this line. Moreover, every workers' committee should be regarded as entitled to all the information now supplied to the shareholder."

While the coal-mining industry under peace conditions had remained strongly competitive, in many industries engaged in the manufacture of standardised products rivalry had already given place to co-operative effort. Before the war such co-operation was almost invariably restricted to the commercial function, the fixing of prices; but there is strong prospect that it will now extend to the manufacturing process. In most cases the Kartel organisation will probably be preferred to trustification. Manufacturing co-operation would secure many economies which have hitherto been lost, and would thus make for industrial efficiency. But a monopolistic association sometimes resulting from such co-operation may be a source of danger to the community, and its policy thus require careful supervision. The majority of the important commercial organisations before the war existed in industries subject to actual or potential foreign competition even in the British market, and so long as the free-trade policy was pursued their power over prices was therefore strictly limited. But the power of the new associations in the near future may become far greater, and the danger of anti-social action more serious.

The remedy is not to be found in legislation preventing the formation of Kartels. These represent a development which tends to economise human effort, and, like technical inventions, may therefore become valuable instruments of progress. The problem is to secure that the general advantages they offer will be enjoyed by the community. The method by which this may best be secured will partly depend (as in coal-mining) upon the nature of the industry. But two things seem to be essential. The first is that the associations should work in the full light of day. The nation cannot afford to allow grievances to accumulate for a number of years before the appointment of commissions of inquiry—such as that on Shipping Conferences (1906–09). The second requirement, which is closely related to the first, is that the Kartel, unlike the German Kartels, which consist of associations of manufacturers only, should contain representatives of the public. It is possible that in the distant future the existing method of forming different combinations of manufacturers for different purposes may give place to a new method, in suitable industries, of forming comprehensive associations, with joint boards of employers and workers' associations—upon which the State will be represented. These Boards would fix both prices and wages, and deal with all matters relevant to the industry. In those standardised industries for which this method will be appropriate the Boards would be the logical outcome of 'Whitley' Councils.

One of the greatest needs of the present is publicity. Competition has hitherto been based largely upon secrecy—secrecy in respect of both method of manufacture and the financial results of the enterprise. The effect of competition has thus been less stimulating than it might have been, and the system has generated suspicion and mistrust among the work people, and possibly an exaggerated idea of the average rate of profits obtained in industry, as distinguished from commerce. Not merely the arithmetical average of profits for an industry, but their 'frequency distribution' should be submitted to the 'Whitley' Councils [1] and afterwards published. The publication of results should not be restricted to highly organised trades. If no organisation exists which could undertake the work it should be done by a public authority. Moreover, failing effective competition the public authority —either the State or municipality—should follow the

[1] That is, *e.g.*, x firms made 10 per cent. on *actual* capital; $(x+3)$ firms made 11 per cent.; $(x+10)$ made 12 per cent., and so on. For this purpose the results should be obtained and stated in the same way, so that they may be strictly comparable; nominal capital should be distinguished from actual capital, etc.

plan adopted during the war (when 'national kitchens' were established) and destroy the quasi-monopoly by becoming itself a competitor. The mere threat of competition by a public authority in the supply of coal, milk or other important commodity, would in most cases be sufficient to maintain prices at a competitive level. There seems little doubt that in many places the co-operative store has done effective work of this character and has thus amply justified its existence.

It seems to me that the solution of the general problem of industrial reorganisation is not to be found in nationalisation. There are cases in which the problem of organising is so difficult that the only way to 'organise' effectively is not to organise at all. For example, no one would suggest world socialism for the simple reason that to attempt to organise on a world basis would be to court disaster. Scarcity and abundance are therefore left to manifest themselves in prices, which in turn react upon the force of competition. It should not be forgotten that organisation involves responsibility at the centre. The greater the area covered by any regulation and the more far reaching its results the more serious the consequences of error. Mistaken effort on the part of a single employer would be of more serious consequence to himself than to the community. An error of the same nature by a central authority would reverberate through the whole industry. The danger of such errors increases with the size of the industry and the number of industries brought under State management. Moreover, the difficulty of control and management increases more than proportionately to an increase in the size of the industry. Adequate devolution, which would effectively decentralise responsibility for ' local ' policy and secure the enlistment of that initiative which centralised administration undoubtedly tends to suppress, would mean the restoration of what is essential in the competitive system.

In strictly competitive industry it seems to me that the true function of the State (or municipality) is to make competition effective, by enforcing publicity, and, where necessary, by becoming itself a competitor. In a standardised industry organised upon a Kartel basis the State would be able to regulate policy not only by enforcing publicity but also by being represented upon the Industrial Board. Further action would be determined by the nature of the specific problem presented by each industry. If, however, an industry is controlled by a monopolistic trust the problem becomes far more difficult. It is no argument that centralised control would be ineffective, for by assumption the industry is already centrally controlled, and the chief disadvantages of State management already exist. A State monopoly is to be preferred to an uncontrolled private monopoly of this character, particularly where the power of the monopoly (and therefore the danger of anti-social action) is increased by the protection offered by import duties. Where, as in the case of tramways, the monopoly is that of a single producing unit, the case for public control is exceptionally strong. If the market is supplied by more than one producing unit, all owned by a monopolistic trust, the remedy seems to lie in the abolition of the trust and the formation of several financial and legal entities, linked together by the formation of a Kartel upon which the State will be represented. The last of these problems (that presented by a monopolistic trust) is not likely to become serious in this country.

One of the most urgent problems is that created by the growth of 'international' trusts domiciled abroad, or international agreements between national trusts or Kartels. A notorious example is the Beef Trust; but there are others. The solution of this problem is not to be found in legislative action by one State. It is essentially a problem calling for co-operative effort on the part of the many States. The remedy should be sought by the economic department of the League of Nations. This will be no simple task. The doctrine of international economic responsibility under peace conditions has not yet been accepted. It would be no easy matter to arouse moral indignation in America against a Beef Trust which dealt leniently with American consumers and mercilessly exploited those nations which imported the products. Nor would it be less difficult to create a feeling of resentment in this country against, say, a British Steel Trust which sold steel abroad at a price far above that which was charged to British consumers.

The example drawn from steel manufacture (though none the less valuable) is purely hypothetical. As there is no immediate danger of an international trust or agreement, the more probable event is that American and German combines will export steel to this country and that we shall export steel products to other countries at prices below specific cost of production, or at least below selling price in the home market. Dumping of this character does not appear to be a net advantage to the importing country if the latter contains a competing industry sufficiently large to supply requirements. The temporary reductions in prices add disproportionately to commercial risks in the competing industry if not, indeed, in the industry using the dumped product as 'raw material.' If this is admitted there is a strong *prima facie* case for anti-dumping legislation, which would forbid the sale of the imported article at a price below that charged to consumers in the producing country. It is extremely likely that, for reasons already given, the problem of dumping will become acute in the metal industries before normal conditions are restored.

It will thus be seen that different industries present different problems, for which no universal solution should be sought. But the attacks upon the competitive system and against profiteering and monopoly arise largely from the feeling, not that any alternative system would be more effective in production, but that it would produce a more equitable distribution of the results of industrial effort. The most serious evils of the present system lie on the distributive rather than the producing side. It is true that a monopolistic combination such as an engineering or motor trust might deliberately restrict production, under given circumstances, in order to increase revenue: but such combinations are rare in this country, nor do the circumstances often arise which make such a policy financially sound. Advocates of nationalisation are usually content to deny that their policy would injure production; they seek to justify it by reference to the enormous improvements likely to be effected in the distribution of the nation's income. Behind all attacks upon the system, and particularly the manner in which it works—or fails to work—at present, lies the feeling that there exists a 'fair wage,' 'just price' and 'reasonable profit.' If the existence of these be assumed it seems to follow that a 'just price' is the price that provides a 'reasonable profit' after payment of a 'fair wage.'

2. The Problem of Joint Control

The problem of distribution will be examined in the last chapter. It is necessary first to refer to the claim that industry should be 'democratised' by the admission of workers to a share in control and management. The problem here is not merely that of reducing hours, raising wages, providing greater continuity of work and improving the objective conditions of employment. It is more than providing security by giving the worker longer terms of engagement and protecting him against capricious action on the part of an employer or his foreman. Improvements of this character are important—perhaps even yet the most important in the minds of the vast majority of industrial workers—but they may be effected by existing organisations. Nor is the problem that of providing equality of opportunity, which would enable some workers to advance to the position of managers or employers. Firms enter into contracts with their workers whereby the latter agree to provide, in return for wages, personal effort under 'expert' supervision. It is held that the status of the worker is inferior to that of the other party to the contract, and should be raised by the application of the democratic principle of self-government; that is, workers *as such* should at least enjoy a far greater measure of control and responsibility than is at present the case, and ultimately either a share or more than a share in management, or in ultimate control, or both. It will thus be seen that the claim represents a vague aspiration rather than, in general, a specific demand.

In considering the question it is desirable to distinguish carefully between private and nationalised industry. Under private enterprise there are many possible forms of 'joint control,' one of which has been in operation for many years. Joint committees of employers' federations and trade unions negotiate agreements which prescribe wages, hours of work and certain objective conditions of employment, and these are frequently supplemented by shop customs which, if not formally 'recognised,' are in practice observed as faithfully as the former. In strongly organised industries the agreements and customs together restrict the 'freedom' or 'sovereignty' of the firm to a considerable extent, and represent the degree of 'control' already enjoyed by the workers. An engineering firm, for example, may be compelled to dismiss some of its engineers, or employ them on short-time on account of a temporary shortage of castings, which cannot immediately be removed merely because the moulders are unwilling—or cannot obtain permission from the union—to work overtime. But this form and degree of control fails to bring satisfaction. In the first place, it generally represents control by the union, not immediate control by the workers in the establishment. The latter feel that they are not a party to the negotiations, and have no voice in the determination of the conditions of their own work. There is strong reason to believe that the demand for control represents, in part, a strong reaction against the centralisation of power in trade union government, and that to that extent it would be satisfied by a greater degree of devolution in trade union administration. In the second place, the degree of control is not sufficient.

The recommendations of the Whitley Committee appear to be designed to meet these objections. In the first place, the organisation which is proposed provides for a greater degree of devolution of function than obtains under the present organisation. The Whitley

Committee recommended the establishment of Joint Industrial Councils, supplemented by District Councils, and these in turn by Works Committees. The principle of devolution is thus fully accepted, and establishment committees become, for the first time, an integral part of the organisation of the industry. That in itself represents an important step in advance. But the proposals have been criticised on the ground that they do not go far enough in the direction of decentralisation. Organisations are jealous of their own powers and delegate as little as possible to others. It is now feared that a tendency towards centralised or ' bureaucratic ' administration would be displayed by the National Industrial Councils. If experience shows the fear to be well grounded, the Whitley scheme is doomed to failure. Over-centralisation leads to local revolt and weakens the sense of obligation under general agreements. This in turn handicaps the leaders and makes them more unwilling to conclude such agreements without resort to the ballot. With constant reference to the electorate representative government becomes government by delegates, who merely act as the mouthpieces of the mass, and true leadership is at a discount. The solution of the difficulty must depend upon the nature of the industry and its problems, the degree of geographic concentration and the influence of tradition.

The second objection urged against the Whitley scheme is that it not merely does not go far enough, but it even perpetuates the existing economic system. It certainly marks a considerable advance upon the Conciliation Boards of the past. These met but infrequently, and generally in an atmosphere already charged with suspicion. The representatives of the two sides only met to consider claims and counterclaims, and thus frequently only knew each other as potential or actual antagonists. Their powers were restricted to deal only with those matters regarding which there was real or supposed conflict of interest. It is idle to pretend that the interests of the two parties are identical. Although they live by serving each other and rendering joint service to the community there is, and must be, a serious conflict of interest between them, whether the employers be regarded as merely a buffer between the worker and the consumer or as a powerful functionary able to take toll of each. But there *are* common interests, and it is an important merit of the Whitley scheme that it aims at providing an organisation for the discussion of such matters. The councils meet at regular and frequent intervals. They should thus deliberate in an atmosphere of peace and goodwill. The agenda may contain anything relevant to the industry. Consequently the success or failure of the scheme will depend upon the spirit in which it is adopted and operated.

National Councils may become valuable instruments of progress, not only adapting themselves to gradually changing and developing conditions, but able to shape such developments ; but if they are regarded merely as slight extensions of the old Conciliation Boards, and their work is conducted in an atmosphere of secrecy and suspicion, they are doomed to failure.

But the most important feature of the Whitley scheme is probably the provision for the establishment of Works Committees. The new claims of 'labour' relate more particularly to the workshop than the industry; and to the relationship of the individual worker to the firm and its representative rather than to the financial reward of the craftsman. The Works Committee, which is intended to improve the status of the worker, is a joint committee for the discussion of problems which arise in the establishment and are integral to that establishment. Here again it may be said that its success will depend upon the spirit in which it is accepted by the firm and the workers, and conducted by its members. Obviously, however, it can be no more than a body for conducting negotiations, concluding agreements and conveying suggestions to the manager. From its very nature it is an unsuitable body for performing important executive functions. The workers' representatives may be able to enforce certain conditions through the employment, if necessary, of economic force—the threat of strike—in precisely the same manner as a trade union may do at a Conciliation Board. The management may take the workers' representatives on the committee into its confidence, even seek advice in matters of difficulty; and the latter may offer helpful suggestions on questions of internal organisation. There are obvious possibilities; and many such committees have more than justified their existence. But many workers seek more than committees of this character. Their claim is a share in management and in the responsibility for the enterprise as a whole.

Committees of workers' representatives were established during the war to negotiate and administer systems of collective bonus, or to perform purely disciplinary functions, such as enforcing regular and punctual attendance. The timekeeping and bonus committees represent a start; but it is contended that they should do more than enforce discipline or administer the details of a collective bonus: they should be given highly responsible functions to perform connected with management. So far, at any rate, there should be ' self-government ' in industry. Under existing conditions the wage-earners employed by a firm represent an industrial community which is denied those opportunities and duties of ' citizenship ' such as they would enjoy in a democracy. The complete democratisation of industry is unattainable for the time being ; but even under the purely competitive system some approximation to democratic control may be secured by the exercise of what may be called a ' creeping function.' Such appears to be the implied argument of the advocates of joint control.

Two observations may be made by way of specific comment upon this claim. The first is connected with the difficulty of defining the term management. Generally it consists of a group of functions which tend to change in form as the organisation grows. Some functions are delegated and others come into existence. Production is carried on by a process of differentiation and integration of function. The majority of the workers are employed on (though not necessarily in manipulating) inanimate objects ; the minority are engaged in supervising and co-ordinating the work of the larger group, and thus deal with people rather than material. This minority is regarded as the group connected with ' management ' ; it comprises mainly the people who are concerned with the ' human factor ' in industry. But these are no less employees of the firm ; nor are they less concerned than the industrial workers to improve the conditions of their own employment. There are also highly specialised workers, such as chemists and technical experts, performing difficult tasks which call for long and expensive training. Obviously the claim for ' joint control ' is not a claim to perform those technical functions calling for highly specialised training. Is it, then, a claim to 'interfere' with the organisation and the supervision of their own work? To a large extent this is already done. Conditions of employment are standardised, to the extent that this is possible for the particular industry, by means of joint agreements between the two associations; and these agreements 'interfere' with what at one time was regarded as the function of management. There are other conditions which are incapable of standardisation for the industry, although they may be standardised or regularised for the establishment. These would naturally be the subject of negotiation at the 'Whitley' Works Committees; and any such regularisation would further 'interfere' with the function of management. It is difficult to see what additional powers in the sphere of internal organisation could be claimed by a shop committee of workers without a complete revolution in the relations of the firm to the workers as a whole. For what is not capable of standardisation but must remain flexible seems to be precisely that which calls for specialised skill and work no less exacting than that of the trained engineer.

The second observation is closely connected with the first. To the extent that we value material progress, the claim to a share in management must finally be based not upon any appeal to 'abstract justice' or 'democratic principle.' Its ultimate strength is determined by the power to provide that service to which the claim is made. A Workers' Committee obviously has no claim to determine in what proportions the constituents of some important chemical product should be combined. If it insisted upon doing so the firm would soon cease to exist. The same argument applies in the case of all specialised functions.

But if such a committee were able to show that it could perform a specific service more effectively than it is already being provided, not only would it be justifying its claim, but the firm would naturally, in its own interests, if for no other reason, delegate that function to the committee. This seems to provide the real test, not only in competitive industry but under all forms of economic control which emphasise the importance of efficiency in production. It is the corollary of specialisation of tasks that each should be performed in the most efficient manner.

If a Workers' Committee is to perform any service effectively, it must accept the obligations attaching to that service. An interesting proposal has recently been made by a group of engineering workmen on the Clyde, which involves a greater degree of control by the workers than any yet specified. Under this scheme (which is locally known as 'Collective Contract' and elsewhere as the 'Fellowship System') all the employees of the firm would form themselves into an association which would enter into a comprehensive contract with the firm for the manufacture of the product at a given price. The firm would supply the raw material and the plant, but exercise no control over manufacture. The manager, the technical experts and all concerned with internal organisation (but not, of course, the directors) as well as skilled and unskilled workers, would be members of the association, which would be represented by a committee to which all would be responsible. Many objections may be urged against this scheme, and these may be at present so weighty that it may be regarded as impracticable, not only in so varied an industry as engineering, but even in those manufacturing industries of which the products are highly standardised. But we are here concerned not with its merits but with its implications. It obviously implies the formation of an association of the nature of a joint-stock company, the members of which are the workers. The managing committee would need to be empowered to enter into contracts, enforceable at law, with the firm for the delivery of the products not only at stated prices but also within stated periods. Failure to fulfil any contract would carry with it penalties, such as are not imposed, under existing conditions, upon the workers. In other words, control of this character cannot be divorced from responsibility.

The difficulty of separating control from responsibility is clearly seen in relation to a claim of a somewhat different character which is frequently made by or on behalf of industrial workers. Workers spend a great part of their life in the factory under conditions laid down by others ; they work in obedience to a policy in the determination of which they enjoy no share. The ultimate control is in the hands of shareholders working through a Board of Directors. It is held that the enterprise should be regarded as a partnership on equal terms between the shareholders and the workers, and that the two groups should have equal representation on the Board. There already exist copartnership schemes under which workers own a proportion of the share capital, and are therefore represented by a director. But they are represented as shareholders, not as workers. The present claim is that they should be represented as workers, and represented to the extent of one-half of the Board.

It is probable that the desire to share ultimate responsibility for the policy of an enterprise now controlled by shareholders whose interest is merely financial and may be of short duration is stronger and more deeply rooted than the desire to share subordinate executive functions. But the ultimate control of policy is vested in the shareholders for the reason that they accept financial responsibility. Workpeople have discounted the major risk of the enterprise by accepting fixed rates of wages guaranteed in theory for the period covered by the wage contract, and in practice for a much longer period. The shareholders enjoy no such guarantee, but accept the hazards of the enterprise. The directors are representatives appointed by their constituents (the shareholders) to conduct the business and to enter into legally enforceable contracts and take all the risks necessary to perform their task in an efficient manner. If, therefore, we assume—as we must assume—that ultimate control and responsibility are inseparable, the workers' directors would require to be empowered by their own constituents to accept joint responsibility and jointly to undertake risks. In other words, wages would no longer be a guaranteed payment but a residual payment varying with the success of the enterprise. As in the last example, the workers would need to form themselves into a subsidiary association of the nature of a joint-stock company, recognised by law as a legal entity against which action might, if necessary, be taken. This association would enter into a working agreement with the complementary association of shareholders for the joint working of the business. The agreement would obviously need to specify the proportions in which the residual amount should be divided between the two groups: for example, it might state that a given standard rate of 'wages' (no longer wages in the ordinary sense of the term) was equivalent to a given standard rate of interest, and that any variation in the surplus (or deficit) would be shared between the parties in a specified ratio. Given an agreement of this character, the subsequent interests of the two groups would be more nearly parallel than they are at present. But there appears to be no prospect either that the workers would accept the responsibilities of control of this character, or, if a proportion did accept them, that a sufficient supply of capital could be attracted to make experiment on a large scale possible. It should be added that if the workers accepted all the responsibilities of the undertaking and gave full security for borrowed capital, they would enjoy exclusive control, and the enterprise would become essentially an ' association of producers ' similar to those which were tried half a century ago. That the latter failed is not a final argument against repeating the experiment.

These important examples of ' control ' by the workers illustrate the difficulty of applying the idea of ' democracy ' to industry organised on a basis of economic freedom. A factory is not a community in the sense that a nation is a community ; strictly speaking, it represents a group of markets in which services, in being rendered, are bought and sold. It is difficult to ' democratise ' contractual relationships, even where the democratic State or Co-operative Society is the employer. Democracy in industry implies the old form of self-governing workshop.

An employing firm which received a request from its employees for a share in control would be justified in asking three questions: " What precisely is the function which you desire to perform ? " " Can you perform it as efficiently as it is performed at present ? " " Are you prepared to accept all the reponsibilities which attach to that function ? " A satisfactory reply to all three would constitute a justification of the request. But even if we assume that a committee of the workers could be trained to exercise the function of control, whether it be that of 'administrative' control within the factory as managers or assistants, or ultimate control of policy as directors, it is at least doubtful whether the demand of the rank and file would be satisfied. "What is desired is that the direction of an industry shall be the affair of *all* the members of that industry, so to speak, *ex officio*; that they, as producers, *i.e.* as men who spend the greater part of their time and strength in an industry, should have, as their normal share in it, the right and the responsibility of participating in the finest and highest of its duties."[1] But what in practice might result is the creation of a new group of specialists whose control would inevitably become 'bureaucratic' and produce a further reaction against the new form of organisation.

This tendency towards bureaucracy would probably be even stronger in a nationalised industry, where the power of the workers is likely to be less than it may be in competitive industry. The proposal for State ownership combined with workers' control, which has recently been put forward from many quarters, represents an endeavour to effect a compromise between 'bureaucratic' Socialism and Syndicalism. We need not here attempt a close discussion of any of these systems. It is sufficient to point out that the State must either be supreme or not supreme. If the supremacy of the democratic State (which is more than a piece of industrial mechanism) is challenged explicitly or by implication; if the sovereignty of the State is limited by the powers enjoyed by the workers; if the workers

[1] *Social Purpose*, by Muirhead and Hetherington, p. 188.

are to enjoy rights *against* the State, rather than rights conferred by the State, the proposal is bound to fail. No democracy would give it acceptance. There can be no limited partnership between the whole and a part. If, on the other hand, the supremacy of the State is admitted, the proposal does not differ essentially from State Socialism—to be strictly correct, the proposal relates merely to the degree of power which should be delegated to the workers by a Socialist State. It merely raises an administrative problem. There is no real *via media* between Socialism and Syndicalism.

It would be foolish to dogmatise about the final outcome of the widespread desire for 'control' by the workers. It is felt with increasing strength that the 'spiritual' value of industry as an 'institution' is insignificant in the case of wage-earners, whose work in most cases provides little or no opportunity for self-expression. But it would be worse than foolish to ignore the difficulties in the way of giving effect to that desire. In the first place, it has not yet been formulated with sufficient precision to enable its practicability to be estimated. "Never can it be too well understood," said Professor Maccunn, "that if men possess ideas, as of course they do, it is not less true that men are possessed by ideas, vitalised by ideas, swept along by ideas, long before the ideas that master them have come to logical clearness and definition."

In the second place, so long as we as members of the community attach so much importance to efficient production that we prefer more material wealth *without* workers' 'control' to less wealth combined *with* such control in its manufacture, the nation will only be prepared to accept that degree of control which is consistent with efficiency. Efficiency means complexity of organisation. The modern tendency is towards increased complexity, and the more complex the organisation the more specialised the function and the greater the need for long and careful training for its exercise. Moreover, the more central the function the greater is its responsibility, and the more serious are the consequences of error in its performance. For this two-fold reason the tendency has been towards delegation of such functions to qualified experts. Control by the workers, if it is to be effective control of important functions, would reverse the tendency produced by the desire for efficient production. This is not to say that efficient production, narrowly interpreted, is a god to be worshipped. But it should be understood in advance that we cannot expect so high a material standard of living with inefficient control by the workers as with efficient control by experts. Nor should it be forgotten that workers' control, if it is to be real in the sense that the term 'real' is commonly understood, would not be control by experts. Under the competitive system a continuous test of individual experiment is provided by the force of competition. A similar experiment conducted simultaneously in all competing firms, or in an industry controlled by a monopoly, or owned and controlled by the State, is subject to no such test.

In the third place, a considerable period must elapse before the workpeople will be prepared to accept the duties and responsibilities which are inseparable from the exercise of the powers of control in private industry. Control of policy involves contract of a new kind and the obligations of such contract; it presupposes the formation of an association competent to accept such obligations ; and implies the abolition of wages as the term is at present understood, the acceptance of new risk, and of a residual payment measuring the success or failure of the enterprise. In publicly owned industries there can be no control of this character, but merely the exercise of functions delegated by a ' superior ' authority representing the State and responsible to the State.

It would therefore appear that the recommendations of the Whitley Committee contain, not all that some of the workpeople desire, but certainly as much as the vast majority of workers are yet prepared to accept in an industry privately organised. The Works Committees represent an advance in two ways, first by securing more effective devolution than was provided in the pre-existing organisation of capital and labour, and secondly by giving new powers to the National Councils and Works Committees. The function of the Works Committee is indeterminate, and may be regarded as including the consideration of further control by the workers themselves. It thus provides an opportunity for the advocate of joint control to translate his ideal into a practical scheme able to survive the searching test of criticism by those already experienced in the task. It also offers training for those likely to exercise some of the controlling functions on behalf of the workers. The Works Committee provides a test and an opportunity. It is in the factory rather than the council chamber of the Conciliation Board that confidence has been undermined or destroyed ; and it is in the factory that it must be restored.

CHAPTER VIII

WAGES AND DISTRIBUTION

IT has frequently been urged on the one side that the only effective method of improving the position of workers is to increase production, and, on the other, that an essential preliminary to any substantial increase in personal efficiency is an improvement in the distribution of wealth by an increase in wages. Both statements contain an element of truth. No substantial and permanent improvement in the position of workers as a whole may be expected without an increase in the mass of goods produced and services rendered in the course of a year. It is futile merely to talk about better housing conditions: the houses must be erected. Better clothes and boots, more meat, vegetables, fruit and other edibles must be provided before they can be consumed. The provision of education is impossible without a supply of teachers and of schools and other requisites. On the other hand, a great deal of labour energy, under peace conditions, was devoted to the making of extravagant luxuries and the provision of armaments for all nations. A mere redirection of effort, without any net increase in personal effort, would have rendered possible a considerable improvement in the position of those groups of workers who were relatively badly paid. But, to erect better houses and provide more food and clothing, without at the same time providing means of payment to those unable to purchase a sufficient supply of necessaries, would not have solved the difficulty. The possible standard of living for the members of the community obviously depends both upon the total production and the categories of goods produced and services rendered. These categories are in turn determined by the way in which the money income is distributed. But it should not be forgotten that such distribution itself affects motive and stimulus, and thus indirectly reacts upon production. Moreover, not only the amount of wages, but also its method of payment, exercises an important effect upon stimulus.

Apart from methods of payment, which have already been discussed, there are clearly two kinds of wages problems. The first relates to the adjustments of the relative rates paid in different occupations, or for different forms and amounts of work. The second relates to the adjustment of the relative payments for personal effort and for investments of capital. The distinction between the two types of problems is important.

It has already been stated that employers offer, and must offer, a rate of pay sufficient to attract an adequate supply of labour. Under strictly competitive conditions, wages rates in different occupations would thus be such as to secure the required distribution of labour over the whole field of employment. They would vary according to the need for training, the objective conditions of employment and other factors ; and the variations would be precisely those which, in the minds of the workers themselves, should exist. In other words, the relative wages which effective competition secured would be accepted as ethically just wages. We found, however, that in practice the competitive force was not so strongly operative as was assumed in theory. In some cases workers were not aware of the rates which the market for their labour would bear, and accepted lower wages than they might have secured if they had possessed greater knowledge and greater power to give effect to such knowledge. In other cases many workers—particularly women workers—were excluded, for various reasons, from large groups of occupations, both industrial and professional. Their competition was therefore concentrated upon a narrow range of (unskilled) occupations, and in that sphere was so intense and individual as to force remuneration below those rates which would have been secured if the competitive area had been enlarged and the workers themselves had possessed greater mobility. In the first group of occupations trades unions have been instrumental in improving the condition of the workers ; in the second, the minimum rates fixed by Boards established under the Coal Mines and Trade Boards Acts have produced similar results. Individual competition, if it was ever an effective force in the sphere of labour, has been supplanted by labour combination over a large range of industries. Rates of remuneration for individuals are fixed by the associations to which they belong. But the problem of adjusting relative rates remains. That problem is, first, to fix the individual rates paid (in the same and in different districts) in a single occupation, and, secondly, to determine the relative rates paid in different occupations.

The principle upon which the first of these is based is that of equal pay for equal work, and the principle is translated into practice by insistence upon a standard minimum rate for a district (but not always the same rate in all districts), efficiency above the normal being recognised by the payment of a rate above the minimum. Thus a trade union does not aim at a uniform rate of payment irrespective of efficiency. Theorists inform us that the result of this policy is the elimination of those who are not worth the minimum, and the consequent increase in the general efficiency of the labour group controlled by the union. The more frequent result in practice (and a result which will become still more common as labour organisation is extended) is that the inefficient people continue to be employed in brisk times and, as far as possible, are dismissed first when depression sets in. They thus remain in the trade; their employment is more precarious than that of the worker of average efficiency, and their total wages over a long period correspondingly lower. Moreover, because they appear to be overpaid, and consequently burdensome to the industry, the tendency (where time-wages prevail) to pay rates above the minimum to the most efficient workers is probably less pronounced than it would otherwise be; and the weaker group thus tend to become a burden upon the stronger group. Finally, the system tends to result in an average individual output within the capacity of a low average worker. Under the Trade Boards Act an individual worker of distinctly lower efficiency than the average may be licensed to work for an employer at a rate below the specified minimum. It is not unlikely that as labour organisation is extended and strengthened, this method will become not merely more desirable socially, but even acceptable to the workmen, exemption by 'licence' being recognised as the corollary of the standard rate, that is, as inherent in the principle of equal pay for equal work. It is probable, indeed, that the problem of wages paid to women employed on work also performed by men will ultimately be solved in this way. The strict meaning of equal pay for equal work (which implies unequal pay for unequal work), is payment according to efficiency. Two workers receive equal *rates* of pay when it is a matter of indifference to the employing body which of the two is employed. And such equality is precisely the result which competition, if it were really effective, would secure.[1]

The problem of adjusting piece-rates to time-rates, though of considerable practical difficulty, raises no question of fundamental principle. It is universally agreed that an average time-worker should do a 'fair' day's work, and that therefore, when employed on piece-work, his weekly earnings should bear some definite relation to his weekly time-rate. What constitutes a reasonable excess or 'balance' is a subject of controversy which is ultimately bound up with the controversy as to what constitutes a fair day's work under a time-wage system. It appears to be generally agreed in skilled engineering that the average piece-worker should be able to earn a balance of between one-quarter and one-third of his time-rate. Apart from any question of 'justice' a smaller prospective balance fails as a stimulus to effort. There appears to be strong evidence, for example, that a contributory cause of the recent reduction in the output of coal is the fact that the advances given to miners have taken the form of flat advances (now amounting to 5s. per day) irrespective of output, thus reducing the percentage balance and considerably weakening the stimulus once provided by payment according to individual output. The translation of

[1] This point is more fully discussed in a memorandum submitted to the War Cabinet Committee on Women's Wages, and published in the volume of evidence.

such advances into tonnage rates would probably result in a considerable increase in total production, provided the minimum day-rate fixed under the Coal Mines Act were raised to such a level that it would bear the same ratio to normal piece earnings as in pre-war days.

The problem of adjusting the relative rates paid in different occupations differs intrinsically from the first. The recent claim of miners for an advance in wages was based upon the view (which the Coal Industry Commission endorsed) that the rates previously paid in the mining industry were low relatively to the rates paid in iron and steel manufacture, engineering and other industries. The 'grades' movement among railway workers arose from the fact that the relative rates of some occupations were unduly low. It is held that the teaching profession is not properly 'placed' in the general grouping of professions and industries. The justification for a legal minimum wage lies in the fact that helpless workers are 'sweated,' that is, that their wages are extremely low relatively to those paid in organised industries. Adjustments such as these are always called for in a dynamic society.

The principle of equal pay for equal work is not one which can be applied in the manner described in the discussion of relative rates paid to individuals in the same occupation; for it is impossible in theory to establish an equation between occupations in respect of difficulty, training, effort and objective conditions. It has already been stated that under strictly competitive conditions the relative rates would be such as would secure a distribution of workers between the various occupations in proportion to the requirements of the latter. Labour combinations, in seeking relative rates which appear to satisfy the canon of 'justice,' are in search of precisely those relative rates which effective competition would produce. Thus, in effect, the advance claimed by the miners was regarded as necessary to secure those total wages which competition would have enforced in order to provide an adequate supply of labour in the mines if alternative industries had been open to the miners.

Those skilled workers who are relatively well paid attach considerable importance not only to a high standard rate, but also to a rate bearing a definite ratio to the rates paid in other occupations. Partly for this reason the abolition of sweating and the raising of unduly low relative rates will prove a difficult problem. A relative advance in the salaries of school teachers will involve an increase in taxation which, it may be assumed, will not fall upon a large proportion of wage-earners. But a relative advance to badly paid workers employed in industries which are economically independent will be followed in many, if not, indeed, most cases by a rise in prices to consumers, the majority of whom are themselves workers, and their dependents. In other words, a rise in the relative money (and real) wages of badly paid workers involves a fall in the relative money wages of other workers, and, other things being equal, a fall in their real wages.[1]

[1] Some readers may deny the truth of the statement that a rise in those wages which are now relatively low, would be followed by a rise in costs and prices. There are cases in which the rise might produce a corresponding increase in efficiency, or result in the introduction of cheaper methods of production ; but these are not likely to be more numerous and important than those cases in which costs would be adversely affected, at least for a time. It is assumed that the necessary adjustments are made without unnecessary delay.

Skilled workers, accustomed to rates, say, 50 per cent. above those of unskilled workers, and observing the advances secured by the latter, and the rise in prices which is frequently the consequence of such advances (though not always recognised or accepted as such), might, in turn, seek a corresponding advance in their own rates. The upward movement would in time extend to all workers, and the real wages of the badly paid groups would be no better than before, unless it be assumed that an advance in all incomes (which leaves their relative amounts unchanged) can secure a general improvement at the expense of the payment made for the use of capital. Even if that assumption (which is examined below) be granted, the position of the badly paid workers relatively to that of other workers will be no better than before.

Thus it may confidently be stated that the abolition of sweating and the necessary improvement in the position of workers who are relatively badly paid cannot be secured without adversely affecting the position of highly organised and relatively well paid wage-earners, as well as those other consumers who are in receipt of salaries and unearned incomes. It is clear, moreover, that the only way in which the existing divergencies between the rates of wages and salaries paid in different occupations can be permanently reduced is by increasing mobility. Mobility is increased by education and by removing the financial barrier to professions and artificial barriers of other kinds to many of the skilled crafts. Barristers who pursue a policy of exclusiveness in respect of their own profession and condemn the monopolistic policy of craft unions are guilty of inconsistency: so too (for examp'e) are boilermakers who seek to control entry into their trade in a somewhat arbitrary manner while condemning barristers for erecting artificial barriers around their own profession.

A trade union which enjoys a monopoly of an important industry may be able to effect a considerable improvement in the position of its members. For this reason it was commonly assumed that if all workers were organised all could share in the benefit, which would thus be secured at the expense of capital. But the experience of the last five years, during which period the time-rates in most important industrial occupations were practically doubled without any substantial increase in the real wages of time-workers, has cast doubt upon the truth of this assumption. The extent to which the position of labour (in the wide sense) can be directly improved at the expense of interest on capital is one of the unsolved problems of economics.[1] In discussing this problem it is desirable, first, to assume highly competitive conditions, and, secondly, to examine the extent to which the provisional conclusions require to be modified when applied to the economic world as we know it. It may further be assumed that the desired adjustments in relative wages have been made.

The net rate of interest on capital (that is, allowance being made for risk and other factors which load the total interest) is determined by the relation of the available supply of capital to the requirements of economic society. Expenditure on wasteful luxuries increases the demand made for capital and, being the negation of economy, reduces the available supply. It thus raises the general rate of interest and the general level of costs and prices. Thrift produces the contrary effect. The experience of the last few years

[1] Most of the economic problems which are of real importance still remain to be solved!

has brought these statements within the sphere of truisms. If we ignore the effect of foreign investments it follows that without any change in wages rates or the collective efficiency of labour the position of wage-earners would be improved by economy on the part of those who enjoy relatively large incomes. The cost of living would fall and the same weekly earnings as before would purchase more of the necessaries and comforts of life. Thus the mere abolition of that degree of luxurious expenditure which is condemned by moralists would secure an economically desirable redistribution of industrial effort. Moreover, an increase in efficiency would be equivalent to an increase in the supply of capital. If, therefore, everybody worked harder and with more efficient instruments, and even received a proportionate increase in remuneration, interest rates, and therefore costs and prices, would fall and real wages would be raised more than proportionately to the rise in money wages. Economy on the part of the relatively rich, and more efficient work by all workers, represent two main lines of progress in an isolated state. But a universal rise in wages and salaries (which, it is assumed, now bear the desired interrelations) without increase in efficiency or change of habit would not be likely to secure any permanent improvement as against interest. During the transitional period their interrelations might be violently distributed. Moreover, until existing instruments of production had to be reinforced, it is possible, though by no means probable, that there would be some gain to labour. Such gain, however, would be transient. New factories, railways, houses, etc., could only be provided at higher—and proportionately higher—money costs. In the long run money capital would be increased at the same proportion as wages and salaries, and as interest rates would not be permanently changed (it is probable they would be raised for a time) total interest would be likewise increased. The tug of war between capital as a whole and labour as a whole would end in a draw, revealed by a rise in general prices proportionate to the advance in wages and salaries.

Competitive forces do not, however, operate in that simple way. They are hampered at every turn by economic friction. The difficulty of arriving at any confident conclusion applicable to all changes in wages and salaries, however small, is due to the fact that we cannot trace with sufficient exactitude the precise nature of this disturbing force, nor estimate its strength at different points. Two important factors, however, call for comment. The first is that a rise in prices may be, and for some years before the war was, due to currency expansion. It was shown in the fifth chapter that during the process of expansion nominal wages lagged behind prices, real wages fell, and the enjoyment of 'excess' profits was a common feature of most of the important industries. Under such conditions a rise in money wages is necessary to restore real wages, and probably achieves its object. The second factor is the need for capital by foreign countries, some of which have been strong competitors for the capital available in this country. Even if, therefore, it be assumed that labour as a whole can tug successfully against capital as a whole in an isolated state, a fall in the general rate of interest in a state forming one of a family would result in a strong tendency towards the exportation of capital to other states, and consequently in scarcity of capital in the first and a rise in the rate of interest. The momentary (though not the ultimate) effect of an export of capital is the same as the effect of the destruction of capital. And interest rates in all modern States move in sympathy. Thus, on the same questionable assumption, the tug of war, if it were to end in favour of labour (in the widest sense), would need to take place simultaneously in all countries.[1]

[1] A further point calls for comment. *Relatively* high wages in a given occupation provide a stimulus to the introduction of new and better methods of production. An advance in the rates (now unduly low) paid for making ladies' blouses by hand worked machines would probably result in a considerable increasable the proportion of blouses of similar quality made by power machines in factories where the costs are no higher. The workers would thus benefit without ' injury ' to the consumers. But, in an isolated state, a *general* advance in wages which affected no change in *relative* wages would produce no such result. But states are not economically isolated ; they stand in the same relation to each other as different regions within a single state. Ironworks in some parts of the country remain profitable, in spite of antiquated methods of production, for the reason that wages rates are relatively low ; in other parts, in spite of relatively high wages rates, they are profitable because the methods of production are vastly superior. Thus relatively high wages rates do not necessarily mean relatively high costs. They stimulate technical progress. In a state where the average wages rates are high relatively to those prevailing in other states with which the first has important trading connections, the organisation of industry is likely to be more efficient than in the others. It is partly for this reason that the manufacturers in the metal and other standardised industries are able to pay relatively high wages and at the same time compete successfully in neutral markets with their foreign rivals, who pay relatively low wages. For the same reason, too, the products of western states frequently compete successfully with those made by badly paid workers in eastern states. It follows that, in theory, the ideal wage rate which should be paid at any time in a given industry subject to foreign competition (either at home or in foreign markets) is that rate which would tax the efforts of manufacturers to the utmost, and compel improvements wherever and whenever possible. If this rate were paid, and at the same time it bore the appropriate relations to the rates paid in other industries in the same state, wages in general would be at the highest level which the circumstances of that state permitted.

The factors already enumerated call for consideration in any estimate of the future of wages. During the war capital was destroyed on a large scale ; a considerable proportion of the labour force was withdrawn from production for the requirements of peace, and imports from foreign countries were severely restricted. The nation's income of goods and services consumed in time of peace was thus enormously reduced. At the same time the currency of the nation was expanded. Prices rose to a level which corresponded to the shortage of goods and the expansion of currency, and wages were raised in the vain endeavour to restore the old standard of living. All belligerent and most neutral states passed through a similar experience. The question naturally arises whether the advances in wages are likely to be permanent, and, if so, whether they will represent a real improvement in the position of labour. Without attempting a complete answer to this question (which would require a separate volume) the following general observations may be made. In the first place, so long as the currency retains its present degree of expansion, relatively to the amount of goods and services now available, the general level of prices will not fall. But an increase in production, without any further net addition to currency, will result in a proportionate reduction of currency, and a consequent fall in prices. This result, which presupposes economy on the part of the State, will signify the contraction, if not the disappearance of excess profits as a characteristic feature of industry, through the restoration of competition on the part of sellers. But the new standard rates of profits will not be the pre-war standard, but a standard reflecting the scarcity of capital and consequent advance in the rate of interest paid on gilt-edged securities. That rate will remain high so long as capital (in the sense of instruments of production) remains scarce. Until, therefore, approximately the pre-war volume of production is restored, the war bonuses will not represent any perceptible advance (in real wages) upon pre-war days. In the second place, when the pre-war production is again forthcoming, it it possible, though by no means certain, that some advance in real wages will be enjoyed by labour. representing the leeway which had yet to be made up at the outbreak of war, when a large proportion of workers were still suffering from the rise in prices due to the increase in gold supplies. Apart from this fact it seems fairly evident that there will be no substantial improvement without considerable improvements in the methods of production and increase in the efficiency of workers on the one side, and, on the other, a reduction in expenditure upon extravagant luxuries and upon armaments. If these are secured the consequent improvement in the position of labour will not be conditioned by the retention of war bonuses. Finally, the retention of war bonuses in full implies a permanent and considerable expansion of currency. But the future of our currency, as was stated in the sixth chapter, is bound up with the future of the currencies of other States, and thus constitutes an international question. An expanded currency is not a sign of financial strength or industrial prosperity. It is generally agreed that some contraction is necessary. But such contraction will be gradual, if crises are to be avoided, and will roughly keep pace with contraction abroad. There appears to be room for considerable contraction without any reduction in war bonuses, provided the pre-war standard of industrial effort is maintained. And this will correspond to the advance in real wages specified above. Any further contraction will necessitate a reduction of money wages (whether they be called standard rates or bonuses), which the international industrial situation will enforce irrespective of the wishes of employers or workmen. But it is possible that before such process of contraction comes into operation there will be some further expansion, due to the competition of central European States for the restricted supply of foodstuffs and raw materials. Such appear to be the central factors governing the present wages situation, which is thus very uncertain.

Since the beginning of 1917 advances in wages have been awarded by the Committee on Production on a national basis, and the National Industrial Conference of this year recommended that the Interim Court of Arbitration should continue to act in the same way, that is, to give awards which should become operative nationally, and which, moreover, would secure that wages varied with the cost of living. This method appears to be the most suitable for dealing with the period of transition. It was also frequently suggested, before the war, that wages agreements should be made more elastic by providing that wages should be automatically controlled by the cost of living. Such a scheme by reducing, if not eliminating the 'time lag,' would probably have enabled us to escape much of the pre-war industrial unrest resulting from the rise in prices. As a permanent regulator of wages it is, however, defective in two respects. First, it ignores the fact that wages and costs are not independent variables, but partial functions. Costs and prices are themselves partly determined by wages rates, which it was proposed should be determined in turn by prices. Secondly, it does not allow for progress. Economy of effort resulting from technological and commercial progress should be reflected in a reduction in prices, without change in wages rates, which, by remaining constant, would enable workers, *qua* consumers, to share the benefit of sucb progress. At the same time as prices rose before the war many important inventions were made and improvements in organisation secured, which, in the absence of the steady expansion of currency between 1897 and 1914 and the steady export of capital would have resulted in a reduction of costs and prices. Consequently if labour was to share in the general industrial progress of that period, wages should have advanced more than prices. There seems little doubt that one of the greatest social needs of the twentieth century is a stable currency, that is, a currency which will enable industrial progress to be quickly and adequately reflected in a corresponding reduction in prices, or, in other words, a currency which would secure a real correlation between real costs, money costs and prices. Such a currency, which does not yet appear to be within sight, would be an international currency. The economist who discovers it will be worthy of a place amongst the greatest scientists and inventors in the world's history.

There are many who regard profit-sharing as a solution of the difficulty created by the ineffectiveness of competition and the instability of currency. Provided the scheme is restricted to individual firms which enjoy excess profits through their own exceptional efficiency, or good fortune in respect of geographic position, there is much to be said in its favour, and if it is wisely administered (see Chapter IV) little to be urged against it. But as a general solution to a general problem it is bound to fail. For if most firms in most industries enjoy permanent excess profits it seems clear that either wages *rates* should be raised to meet the consequent increase in the cost of living, or prices should fall. Nor does the proposal to limit the rate of interest offer any solution. Such limitation would lead to extravagant waste in business administration, and largely reduce, even where it did not abolish, the stimulus to invention and improved organisation. Moreover, it would only be effective where the limited rate would be a guaranteed rate for a long period ; without such guarantee the industry would fail to attract capital. Finally, general limitation of interest (if, in spite of the attractions offered by foreign investments, it were practicable) would necessitate 'rationing' of capital, or alternately, the constant adaptation of the rate on loanable capital to the demand of the community (*i.e.* fixing the rate at such a level that the demand would be restricted to the available supply) which in turn would produce all corresponding changes in the prices of existing investments.

The conclusion which has been reached does not appear at first sight to hold out much hope for the immediate future. If universal trade unionism defeats its own chief end, namely, an increase in the rate of payment for work at the expense of the rate of payment for the use of capital, how, then, is the distribution of wealth to be improved ? It should be observed that what is required is not merely a rise in wages, but a rise in the standard of living. This may be secured in three ways, which are closely related.

The first of these has already been indicated. It consists of more efficient production on the one hand and, on the other, the reduction of expenditure upon useless things. An increase in production per head would result in an increase in weekly wages without proportionate, if any, rise in cost; it would also economise capital and thus tend to reduce the general rate of interest. The substitution of thrift for extravagance would result in an increase in capital and a fall in the rate of interest. Thus, given a stable currency, there would be a gradual fall in prices, relatively to wages, and a rise in real wages or standard of living. The temporary effect of both increased production and economy upon prices would be influenced by the extent to which capital was exported, being *less* if capital were exported on a large scale than if it were exported on a small scale. But in the former case, the ultimate effect would compensate for the surrender of immediate benefits.

In the second place, the standard of living of workers as a whole may be raised by 'socialising' consumption. Public libraries provide a wealth of literature which may be enjoyed by all who are fond of reading; public parks, concerts and all forms of musical and other entertainment, athletic clubs, etc., bring recreation and amusement within the reach of large numbers who would otherwise find life narrow and uninteresting. The cost per head of providing such services, which are of the first importance when regarded in bulk, is enormously reduced when they are 'socialiced.' This leads to the third method by which the standard of living may be raised for the great majority of the community. That method is the provision of public services by the State, their cost being defrayed partly or wholly out of State revenue. An examination of the history of the last half-century shows that we appear to be moving in the direction of modified communism. During the war even the necessaries of life were subsidised, and during the next few years houses will be provided partly out of public funds.

If we ignore these as being emergency measures, there remains the fact that most income-tax payers are allowed abatements in respect of dependents. Such abatements constitute an indirect subsidy to families. Education, public health and social insurance represent a charge upon public funds. It is probable that a comprehensive scheme of unemployment insurance, subsidised by the State, will shortly be initiated. The possibilities of development in this general direction have not been exhausted.

It seems to me that these represent the three main lines of progress in the future. It is important that as regards the last the attention of the State should be concentrated mainly upon the welfare of children. One of the most important measures which could be devised would be a State subsidised insurance scheme making ample provision to families which have suffered through the early death or complete disablement of the breadwinner. The father of a family whose welfare depends upon his health and capacity to find and retain employment naturally feels the burden of his responsibility. But he is haunted by the dread that he may die before his responsibilities are over, and that his family would thereby be reduced to extreme poverty, if not dependence upon charity. Widows of men who were eminent in their day are frequently placed upon the civil pension list. The widows and dependents of soldiers and sailors killed in war are entitled to pensions. In this respect workers (of all grades) should be regarded as soldiers: by working honestly they perform social service. Without discussing the advantages and disadvantages of a comprehensive insurance scheme to cover the risks specified above, it may be suggested not only that it is the corollary of the provisions likely to be made for education, but also that no insurance measure already introduced or foreshadowed would produce such a profound psychological effect as this would be likely to do.

If there is to be further development towards what has been called modified communism, the cost which will be incurred must add to the importance and urgency of the problem of taxation, which has already acquired both as the result of the war. If (as I believe) taxation is to be the instrument for reducing inequalities in the distribution of the good things of life, it must be graded, as far as possible, with that end in view. There is, of course, a limit beyond which income cannot be taxed without the gross amount being seriously reduced. And the injurious effect upon income would not merely mean a reduction rather than increase in the total revenue derived from income taxation beyond that limit, but probably signify a reduction in the national income of goods and services upon which the standard of living depends. When that limit has been reached (but not until then) the public services which are provided from the resulting revenue will represent the extent to which, under the geographic conditions of this country and in the present state of human efficiency, it is possible to raise the standard of living of the nation as a whole. It is the task of the Government to determine where the limit lies.

INDEX